STUFFED!

THE ART OF THE EDIBLE VEGETABLE BOAT

Quick, Healthy, and Delicious...
If You Like Bowls, You'll Love Boats!

Marlena Kur

CREATOR OF *Zest My Lemon*

Race Point
PUBLISHING

Special thanks to Melissa Petitto R.D.

Brimming with creative inspiration, how-to projects, and useful information to enrich your everyday life, Quarto Knows is a favorite destination for those pursuing their interests and passions. Visit our site and dig deeper with our books into your area of interest: Quarto Creates, Quarto Cooks, Quarto Homes, Quarto Lives, Quarto Drives, Quarto Explores, Quarto Gifts, or Quarto Kids.

Text © 2018 by Marlena Kur

First published in 2018 by Race Point,
an imprint of The Quarto Group,
142 West 36th Street, 4th Floor,
New York, NY 10018, USA
T (212) 779-4972 **F** (212) 779-6058
www.QuartoKnows.com

Race Point titles are also available at discount for retail, wholesale, promotional, and bulk purchase. For details, contact the Special Sales Manager by email at specialsales@quarto.com or by mail at The Quarto Group, Attn: Special Sales Manager, 401 Second Avenue North, Suite 310, Minneapolis, MN 55401, USA.

10 9 8 7 6 5 4 3 2 1

ISBN: 978-1-63106-463-0

Editorial Director: Jeannine Dillon
Project Editor: Erin Canning
Photographers: Anett Velsberg-Tiedemann and Marlena Kur (see photography credits, below)
Cover and Interior Design: Jacqui Caulton

Photography by Anett Velsberg-Tiedemann: cover and pages 9, 12, 21, 25, 26, 29, 30, 35, 41, 42, 48, 53, 59, 67, 75, 77, 85, 87, 91, 96, 98, 101, 105, 111, 112, 121, 125, 127, 131, 132, 135, 136, 144, 149, 157, 158, 161, 165, and 166.

Photography by Marlena Kur: pages 17, 36, 56, 63, 70, 72, 78, 88, 94, 114, 116, 122, 142, and 150.

Printed in China

CONTENTS

INTRODUCTION

I have always had a passion for food. As a child, I preferred watching cooking shows to cartoons, and I even began preparing meals for my friends and family at a young age. I dreamed that I would one day become a professional chef and run my own restaurant.

But life doesn't always work out exactly the way you plan. I ended up working in the insurance business for many years, though it was a job I didn't love. When I became pregnant with my third child, I was lucky enough to give up my job in insurance and become a stay-at-home mother. In 2015, I launched my Instagram account, Zest My Lemon (@zestmylemon), which has given me the opportunity to share my easy meal ideas—made with simple ingredients—with the world. In many ways, it has been even better than becoming a professional chef because I get to do what I love every day: raise my children, cook delicious healthy foods, and hopefully inspire others on their journey to clean eating and healthy living. Does it get any better than that?

For those of you who have been following my food journey on Instagram, you may have noticed that I always include an assortment of colorful foods in every meal. Zest My Lemon, at its heart, is a combination of my love for food, art, and creativity. And that's why taking those same nutritional power foods and creating fruit and veggies boats has become such a fun passion for me.

Stuffed fruits and veggies—or "boats," as they're known on Instagram—have helped me get more creative about how I get my daily nutrition. If you eat the same plain avocado or sweet potato every day, it can get boring, fast. By stuffing fruits and vegetables with your favorite flavors and foods, they can become fun, nourishing feasts that fuel you throughout the day. Boats can also help you attain that vital food rainbow, whether you follow a vegetarian diet, low-carb diet, or are just trying to be a little healthier. Take an avocado, potato, zucchini, or pepper, and transform it into a whole new level of deliciousness with the recipes I've created here in my very first book, *Stuffed!*.

So, if you are ready to reinvent the cucumber or power up a sweet potato, then *Stuffed!* is for you! With quick and healthy no-fuss recipes for a satisfying snack, side dish, or nourishing meal at any time of the day, these boats are sure to be a crowd-pleaser for your guests or a fun treat for your kids, and the perfect way to mix up your menu, tantalize your taste buds, and help you get your "five a day."

I hope you enjoy this cookbook, and it inspires you to experiment with your own fruit and veggie boats at home!

—Marlena Kur, creator of Zest My Lemon

Pepper Boats

Hummus and Crudités Bell Pepper Boats   8

Curry Chicken Salad Bell Pepper Boats   10

Ratatouille-Stuffed Bell Pepper Boats   11

Spicy Moroccan Carrot Salad with Yogurt Sauce
Bell Pepper Boats   13

Lentil and Cauliflower Rice–Stuffed
Bell Peppers   15

Green Pepper Egg Bakes   16

Mini Pepper Tuna Bites   18

Cheesy Chicken and Black Bean–Stuffed
Poblano Peppers   19

Philly Cheesesteak Bell Pepper Boats   20

Hummus and Crudités Bell Pepper Boats

TOTAL TIME: 15 minutes
YIELD: serves 8 as a starter

Ingredients
1 can (15.5 ounces, or 439 g)
   chickpeas, rinsed and drained
½ cup (120 g) tahini
¼ cup (60 ml) water
1 tablespoon (6 g) lemon zest
½ cup (120 ml) freshly squeezed
   lemon juice
2 cloves garlic
1 tablespoon (15 ml) ground cumin
1 teaspoon sea salt
¼ cup (60 ml) extra-virgin
   olive oil
4 large red bell peppers
½ cup (68 g) pine nuts, toasted
1 teaspoon paprika
4 large heirloom carrots, peeled
   and sliced
4 ribs celery, cut into 3-inch
   (7.5 cm) pieces
8 radishes, sliced
24 cherry tomatoes

1. In a food processor or blender, combine the chickpeas, tahini, water, lemon zest, lemon juice, garlic, cumin, and sea salt. Puree on high speed until smooth. With the motor still running, add the olive oil and continue to puree until creamy, about 2 minutes.

2. Cut the peppers in half through the stem and remove the ribs and seeds. Pour the hummus into the bell pepper halves. Sprinkle with the pine nuts and paprika.

3. To serve, arrange the crudités (carrots, celery, radishes, and tomatoes) in the 8 boats.

Curry Chicken Salad Bell Pepper Boats

TOTAL TIME: 20 minutes
YIELD: serves 4 as a main course

Ingredients

1 rotisserie chicken, skin removed
 and meat shredded
¾ cup (175 g) mayonnaise
⅓ cup (80 ml) white wine vinegar
⅓ cup (85 g) mango chutney
3 tablespoons (19 g) curry powder
1 cup (110 g) thinly sliced celery
1 cup (150 g) halved red grapes
¼ cup (31 g) sliced almonds,
 toasted
Salt and pepper, to taste
4 large yellow, red, or orange
 bell peppers
¼ cup (25 g) chopped scallions,
 for garnish

1. Place the shredded chicken in a large bowl. Set aside.

2. In a blender, combine the mayonnaise, vinegar, chutney, and curry powder. Blend until smooth and then pour over the shredded chicken.

3. Add the celery, grapes, almonds, and salt and pepper. Stir to combine.

4. Slice each bell pepper in half. Remove the stem, ribs, and seeds. Scoop the chicken salad into the 8 boats and top with the scallions.

Ratatouille-Stuffed Bell Pepper Boats

PREP TIME: 20 minutes
COOK TIME: 1 hour
YIELD: serves 4 as a side dish

Ingredients
Nonstick cooking spray
4 large bell peppers plus 1 large
   red bell pepper, diced (½-inch,
   or 13 mm, pieces), divided
1 medium sweet onion, chopped
2 cups (175 g) diced eggplant
   (½-inch, or 13 mm, pieces)
1 cup (124 g) diced zucchini
   (½-inch, or 13 mm, pieces)
¼ cup (60 ml) plus 1 tablespoon
   (15 ml) olive oil, divided
1 tablespoon (16 g) anchovy paste
2 cloves garlic, minced
1 can (28 ounces, or 794 g)
   diced tomatoes
½ teaspoon dried oregano
½ teaspoon dried thyme
¼ teaspoon fennel seeds
½ cup (30 g) thinly sliced
   fresh basil leaves
Salt and pepper, to taste
½ cup (40 g) shredded
   Parmesan cheese, for garnish

1. Preheat the oven to 400°F (200°C). Line 2 baking sheets with parchment paper. Spray a 9 × 9-inch (23 × 23 cm) baking dish with nonstick cooking spray.

2. Cut the tops off the 4 whole bell peppers, remove the ribs and seeds, and place the peppers in the baking dish. Transfer to the oven and bake for 25 minutes.

3. Arrange the onion and eggplant in a single layer on one of the prepared baking sheets, and the zucchini and diced bell pepper in a single layer on the other. Drizzle the vegetables with ¼ cup (60 ml) of the olive oil. Transfer the baking sheets to the oven and bake for 20 minutes. Remove from the oven and leave the oven on.

4. Once the vegetables are roasted, add the remaining 1 tablespoon (15 ml) oil to a large pot over medium heat. Add the anchovy paste and garlic, and cook and stir for 2 minutes.

5. Add the tomatoes, oregano, thyme, and fennel seeds. Cook, stirring occasionally, for 10 minutes. Add the roasted vegetables and basil, and season with salt and pepper.

6. Spoon the ratatouille into the 4 cooked boats. Top with the shredded Parmesan, return to the oven, and broil until the cheese is melted and bubbly, about 3 minutes. Serve immediately.

Spicy Moroccan Carrot Salad with Yogurt Sauce Bell Pepper Boats

PREP TIME: 20 minutes
COOK TIME: 20 minutes
YIELD: serves 8 as a salad

Ingredients

FILLING

2 pounds (907 g) carrots, peeled and sliced into rounds

¼ cup (60 ml) olive oil

2 shallots, minced

4 cloves garlic, minced

1 tablespoon (15 ml) sugar

1½ tablespoons (23 ml) champagne vinegar

1 tablespoon (14 g) chopped preserved lemon

1 serrano chile, minced (seeded for less heat)

2 scallions, minced

1 teaspoon paprika

1 teaspoon ground cumin

½ teaspoon ground coriander

½ teaspoon ground cinnamon

¼ teaspoon ground ginger

⅛ teaspoon ground cloves

Salt and pepper, to taste

BOATS

4 large yellow bell peppers

SAUCE

½ cup (115 g) nonfat Greek yogurt

¼ cup (60 g) freshly squeezed lemon juice

¼ cup (15 g) chopped cilantro

Salt and pepper, to taste

continued

1. **To make the filling:** Bring a large pot of salted water to a boil. Add the carrots and cook until tender-crisp, 8 to 10 minutes. Drain and allow to dry while starting the rest of the salad.

2. Heat the olive oil in a large skillet over medium heat. Add the shallots and cook until lightly browned and tender, about 5 minutes. Add the garlic and stir until fragrant, about 30 seconds.

3. Stir in the cooked carrots, sugar, vinegar, preserved lemon, chile, scallions, paprika, cumin, coriander, cinnamon, ginger, and cloves. Cook, stirring frequently, for an additional 3 minutes. Remove from the heat, season with salt and pepper, and allow to cool.

4. **To prepare the boats:** Slice the peppers in half through the stem and remove the ribs and seeds.

5. **To make the sauce:** In a medium bowl, whisk together the yogurt, lemon juice, and cilantro. Season with salt and pepper.

6. To serve, spoon the carrot salad into the 8 boats and drizzle with the sauce.

Lentil and Cauliflower Rice-Stuffed Bell Peppers

— fork illustration —

PREP TIME: 15 minutes
COOK TIME: 35 minutes
YIELD: serves 4 as a main course or 8 as a side dish

Ingredients

4 large bell peppers
2 tablespoons (30 ml) olive oil,
   plus more for brushing
1 cup (160 g) chopped onions
2 plum tomatoes, diced
2 or 3 cloves garlic, finely chopped
2½ cups (284 g) frozen riced
   cauliflower
1½ cups (300 g) cooked lentils
   (I use canned)
1 cup (245 g) tomato sauce
Salt and pepper, to taste

1. Preheat the oven to 400°F (200°C). Line a baking sheet with parchment paper.

2. Cut the bell peppers in half lengthwise, keeping the stems intact on one side of each pepper. Remove the ribs and seeds. Place the peppers on the prepared baking sheet at least 2 inches (5 cm) apart. Brush with a little olive oil, inside and out, and bake for 15 minutes. Remove from the oven and let cool for a few minutes before filling. Leave the oven on.

3. Meanwhile, in a large skillet over medium-high heat, heat the 2 tablespoons (30 ml) olive oil until hot but not smoking. Add the onion and tomatoes, and cook, stirring occasionally, until the veggies start to soften, 4 to 5 minutes. Add the garlic and continue to cook for 3 to 4 minutes more. Use a fork to mash and break up the tomatoes into the onion and garlic.

4. Add the cauliflower rice to the skillet. Continue to cook until the cauliflower is softened and well combined with the vegetables, another 4 to 5 minutes.

5. Add the lentils and tomato sauce to the mixture and cook until fully heated, an additional 2 minutes. Season with salt and pepper. Remove the skillet from the heat.

6. Stuff each of the 8 boats with as much of the veggie mixture as possible, heaping it over the tops. Place the peppers back into the oven and bake until the tops begin to brown, 10 to 15 minutes. (You can also broil them for several minutes if you like an extra-toasty top.) Serve warm.

Green Pepper Egg Bakes

PREP TIME: 10 minutes
COOK TIME: 15 minutes
YIELD: serves 4 as a main course

Ingredients
2 green bell peppers, mostly round
Olive oil, for brushing
Salt and pepper, to taste
½ cup (50 g) grated Parmesan
    cheese, divided
4 large eggs
¼ cup (25 g) thinly sliced scallions,
    for garnish

1. Preheat the oven to 400°F (200°C). Line a baking sheet with parchment paper.

2. Cut the stems off the tops of the peppers as close as possible to the top of the pepper without piercing it. (You want to avoid creating a hole where the egg could leak out.) Cut the bell peppers in half lengthwise. Remove the ribs and seeds.

3. Brush each pepper, inside and out, with olive oil, sprinkle with salt, and transfer to the prepared baking sheet. Bake for 5 minutes.

4. Remove the peppers from the oven. If necessary, adjust the peppers to be level on the baking sheet to prevent any egg from pouring over the sides. You can place a piece of folded aluminum foil underneath the pepper as a wedge to level it out. Sprinkle 1 tablespoon (5 g) Parmesan cheese into each pepper half, and then crack an egg into the center of each pepper. Place back into the oven and bake until the whites are fully cooked and the yolks are runny, 8 to 10 minutes.

5. To serve, top the 4 boats with the scallions, salt, and pepper.

Mini Pepper Tuna Bites

TOTAL TIME: 15 minutes
YIELD: serves 8 as a snack

Ingredients

1 can (5 ounces, or 142 g) wild
    albacore tuna, drained
¼ cup (40 g) finely chopped
    red onion
½ cup (50 g) finely chopped celery
2 tablespoons (28 g) mayonnaise
    or 3 tablespoons (38 g) Greek
    yogurt
Squeeze of fresh lemon juice
Salt and pepper, to taste
8 mini sweet peppers
Salad greens (optional),
    for serving

1. In a medium bowl, flake the tuna with a fork.

2. Add the onion, celery, mayonnaise, and lemon juice, and season with salt and pepper.

3. Slice the mini peppers in half lengthwise and remove the ribs and seeds. Stuff the 16 bowls with the tuna salad mixture.

4. Serve on top of the salad greens (if using).

Cheesy Chicken and Black Bean-Stuffed Poblano Peppers

PREP TIME: 20 minutes
COOK TIME: 30 minutes
YIELD: serves 3 as a main course or 6 as a side dish

Ingredients

6 poblano peppers of equal size
2 tablespoons (30 ml) olive oil,
   plus more for brushing
1 pound (454 g) ground organic
   chicken
1 tablespoon (15 ml) chili powder
1½ teaspoons ground cumin
1 teaspoon garlic powder
Salt and pepper, to taste
1 medium yellow onion, roughly
   chopped
1 cup (6 ounces, or 172 g) canned
   black beans, drained and rinsed
½ cup (58 g) shredded Cheddar
   cheese
½ cup (60 g) shredded mozzarella
   cheese
Handful cilantro, roughly chopped,
   for garnish

1. Preheat the oven to 425°F (220°C). Line a baking sheet with parchment paper.

2. Cut the poblano peppers in half lengthwise, keeping the stems intact on one side of each pepper. Remove the ribs and seeds from the center. Place the peppers, cut side down, on the prepared baking sheet, at least 1 inch (2.5 cm) apart. Brush the tops with a little olive oil and bake for 10 minutes. Remove from the oven and set aside.

3. Meanwhile, in a medium skillet over medium heat, cook the ground chicken until brown. Add the chili powder, cumin, and garlic powder, and season with salt and pepper. Continue to cook, stirring occasionally, for another 2 to 3 minutes and then set aside.

4. In a separate medium skillet, heat 2 tablespoons (30 ml) olive oil over medium heat until hot but not smoking. Add the onion and cook, stirring occasionally, until the onions become brown and caramelized, 10 to 12 minutes. Add the chicken mixture to the onions, then stir in the black beans. Cook until heated through, another 2 to 3 minutes. Remove from the heat.

5. Increase the oven temperature to broil. Flip the peppers over, so the cut side is facing up, and gently spread out the edges to create more space for the filling. Spoon as much of the chicken mixture into the peppers as possible, heaping it over the tops.

6. In a small bowl, combine the shredded cheeses. Top the 12 stuffed peppers with a generous amount of the cheese. Transfer the peppers back into the oven and broil until the cheese is fully melted, 2 to 3 minutes.

7. To serve, top with the cilantro.

Philly Cheesesteak Bell Pepper Boats

~~~~~~

PREP TIME: 25 minutes
COOK TIME: 30 minutes
YIELD: serves 4 as a main course

Ingredients
Nonstick cooking spray
4 large green or red bell peppers
1 pound (454 g) rib-eye steak,
    frozen for 2 to 3 hours
2 tablespoons (30 ml) olive oil
1 tablespoon (15 g) unsalted butter
2 cups (230 g) thinly sliced
    sweet onion
1 cup (70 g) sliced cremini
    mushrooms
2 cloves garlic, minced
Salt and pepper, to taste
8 slices extra-sharp provolone

1. Preheat the oven to 350°F (180°C). Spray a 9 × 13-inch (23 × 33 cm) baking dish with nonstick cooking spray.

2. Cut the peppers in half through the stem, remove the ribs and seeds, and place them in the prepared baking dish. Transfer the dish to the oven and bake until the peppers are tender, about 20 minutes. Set aside.

3. Meanwhile, slice the frozen steak as thinly as possible and set aside.

4. Heat a large skillet over medium-high heat. Add the olive oil and butter. Once the skillet is hot, add the onions and mushrooms, and stir and cook until browned, 7 to 10 minutes. Add the garlic, and stir and cook for 30 seconds more.

5. Stir in the thinly sliced beef and cook until browned and cooked through, about 5 minutes. Season with salt and pepper.

6. Increase the oven temperature to broil. Cut the slices of provolone in half and lay a half slice on the inside of each of the 8 boats. Spoon the meat mixture on top and then top with another half slice of cheese.

7. Transfer the peppers back to the oven and broil until the cheese is melted, browned, and bubbly, about 2 minutes.

Cucumber Boats

Chopped Greek Salad Cucumber Boats   24

Couscous, Roasted Tomato, and Goat Cheese Cucumber Boats   27

Burnt Eggplant, Tahini, and Pomegranate Cucumber Boats   28

Falafel, Cucumber-Tomato Salad, and Tzatziki Cucumber Boats   31

Saffron Chicken with Fennel Salad Cucumber Boats   33

Lobster Roll Cucumber Boats   37

Chopped Greek Salad Cucumber Boats

TOTAL TIME: 30 minutes
YIELD: serves 8 as a salad

Ingredients
BOATS
4 English cucumbers

DRESSING
1 teaspoon Dijon mustard
1 teaspoon honey
1 teaspoon dried oregano
¼ teaspoon garlic powder
¼ teaspoon onion powder
2 tablespoons (30 ml) red wine
    vinegar
¼ cup (60 ml) extra-virgin
    olive oil
Salt and pepper, to taste

FILLING
2 romaine hearts, chopped
1 cup (150 g) chopped red and
    yellow bell pepper
1 cup (150 g) chopped cherry
    tomatoes
1 cup (135 g) chopped cucumbers
½ cup (50 g) chopped Kalamata
    olives
½ cup (75 g) crumbled feta cheese
¼ cup (29 g) thinly sliced red onion
¼ cup (15 g) chopped fresh parsley
4 pepperoncini, chopped

1. **To prepare the boats:** Slice the cucumbers in half lengthwise and scoop out some of the flesh, creating a stable boat. Set aside.

2. **To make the dressing:** In a jar, combine all the dressing ingredients and shake vigorously until well blended. Season with salt and pepper.

3. **To make the filling:** On a large cutting board, combine all the filling ingredients and pour the dressing over the top. Finely chop the salad. Divide it among the 8 boats. Serve immediately.

Couscous, Roasted Tomato, and Goat Cheese Cucumber Boats

~~~~~~

PREP TIME: 15 minutes
COOK TIME: 45 minutes
YIELD: serves 8 as a side dish

Ingredients
ROASTED TOMATOES
2 cups (300 g) halved cherry
    tomatoes
1 tablespoon (15 ml) olive oil
Salt and pepper, to taste

DRESSING
1 tablespoon (15 g) Dijon mustard
1 teaspoon honey
2 tablespoons (30 ml) freshly
    squeezed lemon juice
3 tablespoons (45 ml) extra-virgin
    olive oil
Salt and pepper, to taste

FILLING
1 tablespoon (15 ml) olive oil
1 cup (180 g) Israeli couscous
2 cups (475 ml) water
Salt and pepper, to taste
2 cups (40 g) wild arugula leaves
1 cup (20 g) torn basil leaves

BOATS
4 English cucumbers
½ cup (75 g) crumbled goat cheese,
    for garnish

1. Preheat the oven to 300°F (150°C). Line a baking sheet with parchment paper.

2. **To make the roasted tomatoes:** Arrange the cherry tomatoes, cut side down, on the prepared baking sheet. Drizzle with the olive oil and season with salt and pepper.

3. Transfer the tomatoes to the oven and bake until dried and slightly shriveled, 30 to 45 minutes. Meanwhile, make the dressing and filling.

4. **To make the dressing:** In a jar, combine the mustard, honey, lemon juice, and olive oil. Shake vigorously until combined and season with salt and pepper.

5. **To make the filling:** Heat the olive oil in a medium saucepan over medium-high heat. Add the couscous and cook, stirring frequently, until toasted and lightly golden brown, about 2 minutes. Add the water, bring to a boil, and then reduce the heat to low and simmer, covered, for 10 minutes. Turn off the heat and allow to sit, covered, for 5 minutes. Season with salt and pepper.

6. In a large bowl, toss the warm couscous with the arugula, basil, and dressing.

7. **To assemble the boats:** Cut each cucumber in half lengthwise and scoop out some of the flesh, creating a stable boat. Divide the salad among the 8 boats and then arrange the roasted tomatoes and crumbled goat cheese on top. Serve immediately.

Burnt Eggplant, Tahini, and Pomegranate Cucumber Boats

PREP TIME: 20 minutes
COOK TIME: 45 minutes
YIELD: serves 8 as a starter or side dish

Ingredients

1 large Italian eggplant
½ cup (120 g) tahini
1 tablespoon (15 ml) ground cumin
1 tablespoon (6 g) lemon zest
¼ cup (60 ml) freshly squeezed
    lemon juice
¼ cup (10 g) cilantro leaves
1 teaspoon sea salt
4 English cucumbers
½ cup (45 g) pomegranate arils
1 teaspoon Maldon sea salt
1 tablespoon (15 ml) extra-virgin
    olive oil
Pita chips or crudités, for serving

1. Preheat the oven to 425°F (220°C). Line a baking sheet with parchment paper.

2. Pierce the eggplant all over with a knife and place it on the prepared baking sheet. Transfer to the oven and roast for 30 to 45 minutes, turning the eggplant over halfway through the cooking time. The eggplant should be browned and very soft. Allow to cool for 10 minutes.

3. In the bowl of a food processor, combine the tahini, cumin, lemon zest, lemon juice, cilantro, sea salt, and the flesh of the roasted eggplant. (Discard the skin.) Pulse 10 to 15 times, or until the eggplant is chopped and the mixture is well combined. Do not overmix.

4. Cut each cucumber in half lengthwise and scoop out some of the flesh, creating a stable boat. Divide the eggplant mixture among the 8 boats, top with the pomegranate arils and Maldon salt, and drizzle with the olive oil. Serve with pita chips or crudités for dipping.

Falafel, Cucumber-Tomato Salad, and Tzatziki Cucumber Boats

PREP TIME: 20 minutes
COOK TIME: 30 minutes
YIELD: serves 4 as a main course or 8 as a starter

Ingredients

BOATS
4 English cucumbers (see Note, right)

TZATZIKI
1 cup (230 g) nonfat Greek yogurt
1 teaspoon lemon zest
2 tablespoons (30 ml) freshly squeezed lemon juice
¼ cup (15 g) chopped fresh mint
Salt and pepper, to taste

FALAFEL
1 can (15.5 ounces, or 439 g) chickpeas, drained and rinsed
2 cloves garlic, crushed
¼ cup (40 g) diced sweet onion
½ cup (15 g) fresh parsley
½ teaspoon sea salt
1½ teaspoons ground cumin
½ teaspoon crushed red pepper flakes

½ teaspoon dried mint
1 tablespoon (15 g) tahini
1 teaspoon freshly squeezed lemon juice
1 teaspoon baking powder
3½ tablespoons (26 g) all-purpose flour
2 cups (475 ml) olive or vegetable oil

CUCUMBER-TOMATO SALAD
2 Persian cucumbers, chopped (see Note, right)
1½ cups (225 g) quartered grape tomatoes
¼ cup (15 g) chopped fresh parsley
2 tablespoons (30 ml) freshly squeezed lemon juice
1 tablespoon (15 ml) extra-virgin olive oil
Salt and pepper, to taste

Note: English cucumbers are seedless and are longer than Persian cucumbers.

continued

1. **To prepare the boats:** Cut the English cucumbers in half lengthwise and scoop out and reserve some of the flesh, creating a stable boat. Set the boats aside.

2. **To make the tzatziki (make the tzatziki first to allow the flavors to meld):** In the bowl of a food processor, combine the reserved cucumber flesh and seeds, yogurt, lemon zest, lemon juice, and mint. Process for about 15 seconds, or until smooth. Season the tzatziki with salt and pepper, cover, and let marinate in the refrigerator while you make the falafel.

3. **To make the falafel:** Pulse the chickpeas, garlic, onion, parsley, salt, cumin, red pepper flakes, mint, tahini, and lemon juice in a food processor until a rough paste forms. Add the baking powder and flour and pulse until well combined.

4. Heat the oil in a large, deep skillet over medium-high heat for 2 to 3 minutes. Working in batches, carefully drop the falafel batter by the heaping tablespoonful into the hot oil (this recipe makes about 16 falafel). Fry until golden, 1½ to 2 minutes per side. Transfer to a paper towel–lined plate to drain. Repeat with the remaining falafel. Keep warm in a low-heated oven until ready to serve.

5. **To make the cucumber-tomato salad:** In a medium bowl, combine the Persian cucumbers, tomatoes, parsley, lemon juice, and olive oil. Season with salt and pepper.

6. To assemble, arrange the 8 boats on a platter, spoon the salad into the boats, top with the falafel, and drizzle with the tzatziki sauce. Serve immediately.

Saffron Chicken with Fennel Salad Cucumber Boats

TOTAL TIME: 35 minutes
YIELD: serves 4 as a main course or 8 as a starter

Ingredients

1 rotisserie chicken, skin removed and meat shredded

DRESSING

1 cup (230 g) Greek yogurt

2 tablespoons (30 ml) freshly squeezed lemon juice

1 shallot, minced

1 teaspoon Aleppo pepper, see Note, below (or substitute crushed red pepper flakes)

½ teaspoon saffron threads

Salt and pepper, to taste

Note: Aleppo pepper is a Mediterranean chile pepper with a smoky raisin flavor. If you don't have Aleppo pepper, you can mimic the flavor by combining ¼ teaspoon cayenne pepper with ¾ teaspoon sweet paprika.

SALAD

2 cups (40 g) fresh mixed herbs (such as basil, cilantro, chervil, parsley, fennel fronds, and/or dill)

1 cup (90 g) thinly shaved fennel bulb

1 tablespoon (15 ml) freshly squeezed lemon juice

1 tablespoon (15 ml) extra-virgin olive oil

Salt and pepper, to taste

BOATS

4 English cucumbers

continued

1. Place the shredded chicken in a large bowl. Set aside.

2. **To make the dressing:** In a medium bowl, combine the yogurt, lemon juice, shallot, and Aleppo pepper. Crush the saffron threads between your fingers, rubbing them together to release the oils, and add to the yogurt. Whisk to combine and season with salt and pepper. Pour the dressing over the chicken, toss to coat, and let sit for 10 to 20 minutes to allow the flavors to develop.

3. **To make the salad:** In a large bowl, combine the fresh herbs and shaved fennel. Drizzle with the lemon juice and olive oil, and season with salt and pepper.

4. **To assemble the boats:** Cut the cucumbers in half lengthwise and scoop out some of the flesh, creating a stable boat. Spoon the chicken mixture into the 8 boats and top with the salad. Serve immediately.

Lobster Roll Cucumber Boats

~~~~~~

PREP TIME: 25 minutes
COOK TIME: 25 minutes
YIELD: serves 4 as a main course

Ingredients
4 lobster tails (4 to 5 ounces,
    or 113 to 142 g, each)
Garlic powder, to taste
Salt and pepper, to taste
Juice of 2 lemons, divided
Extra-virgin olive oil, for drizzling
2 ribs celery, chopped (about
    ½ cup, or 50 g)
1 bunch scallions, chopped
    (about ¼ cup, or 25 g)
2 tablespoons (20 g) finely chopped
    red onion
¼ cup (15 g) fresh parsley,
    roughly chopped, plus additional
    for garnish
2 tablespoons (6 g) fresh dill,
    roughly chopped
3 to 4 tablespoons (42 to 56 g)
    mayonnaise
4 large cucumbers, any type

1. Preheat the oven to 350°F (180°C).

2. With a sharp knife, slice down the center of each lobster tail, so that the meat is exposed. Season with garlic powder, pepper, a squeeze of lemon, and a drizzle of olive oil. Loosely wrap each tail in aluminum foil, leaving a little room for the lobster to steam within the foil packet. Place on a baking sheet, transfer to the oven, and bake until the lobster is pink and tender, about 25 minutes. (If you like the claw meat and prefer a full steamed lobster, follow the same steps as for preparing the tails but reduce the cooking time to 15 minutes.) Set the lobster aside to cool.

3. Once the lobster is cooled, remove as much meat from the shell as possible using a claw cracker or a nutcracker if necessary. Transfer the lobster meat to a large bowl.

4. Break up the lobster meat, leaving some large chunks. Add the celery, scallions, red onion, parsley, dill, remaining lemon juice, and mayonnaise, and combine well. Season with salt and pepper.

5. Slice each cucumber in half lengthwise and scoop out the seeds, creating a stable boat. Season with salt and pepper. Fill each of the 8 boats with as much of the lobster salad as possible. Garnish with fresh chopped parsley.

Eggplant Boats

Eggplant Parmesan Boats   40

Eggplant and Farro Caponata-Stuffed
Eggplant Boats   43

Quinoa, Mushroom, Spinach, and Tomato-Stuffed
Eggplant Boats with Turmeric Tahini   45

Lamb Gyro-Stuffed Eggplant Boats   46

Roasted Eggplant Boats with Soba Noodles
and Mango Salad   49

Creamed Corn Eggplant Boats   51

Eggplant Parmesan Boats

PREP TIME: 20 minutes
COOK TIME: 20 minutes
YIELD: serves 4 as a main course

Ingredients

4 small eggplants

2 tablespoons (30 ml) extra-virgin olive oil

½ cup (80 g) finely chopped yellow onions

1 cup (150 g) halved cherry tomatoes

3 or 4 cloves garlic, finely chopped

Salt and pepper, to taste

2 cups (490 g) tomato sauce

2 cups (230 g) bread crumbs

8 ounces (227 g) fresh mozzarella cheese, thinly sliced, or 2 cups (230 g) shredded mozzarella

Handful fresh flat-leaf parsley, roughly chopped, for garnish

1. Preheat the oven to 400°F (200°C). Line a baking sheet with parchment paper.

2. Cut the eggplants in half lengthwise. Slice the flesh lengthwise and sideways into squares without piercing the skin. Scoop the eggplant squares out of the skin and transfer to a medium bowl.

3. In a large skillet over medium-high heat, heat the olive oil. Add the eggplant, onion, tomatoes, and garlic. Season with salt and pepper, and cook, stirring occasionally, until the vegetables start to soften, 5 to 7 minutes. Remove from the heat and set aside.

4. Place the 8 eggplant boats onto the prepared baking sheet. Evenly fill each one with the eggplant mixture, then top each boat with about ¼ cup (61 g) tomato sauce. Add the bread crumbs, about ¼ cup (30 g) per boat. Then top with the mozzarella cheese, transfer to the oven, and bake until the cheese is melted and the tops are toasty, 10 to 12 minutes.

5. Garnish with the fresh parsley and season with salt and pepper.

Eggplant and Farro Caponata-Stuffed Eggplant Boats

~~~~~~~~~~~~~~~~~~~~~~~~~~~~~~~

PREP TIME: 20 minutes
COOK TIME: 1 hour 15 minutes
YIELD: serves 4 as a main course

Ingredients
Nonstick cooking spray
2 medium eggplants
¾ cup (120 g) dry farro
2 tablespoons (30 ml) olive oil,
    divided
2 ribs celery, diced
1 cup (160 g) diced red onion
6 ounces (170 g) pitted green
    olives, quartered
¼ cup (34 g) rinsed and drained
    capers
¼ cup (65 g) tomato paste
½ cup (120 ml) red wine vinegar
2 tablespoons (30 ml) sugar
½ cup (63 g) sliced almonds,
    toasted and chopped
¼ cup (15 g) thinly sliced
    fresh basil
¼ teaspoon sea salt
½ teaspoon freshly ground
    black pepper
½ cup (55 g) torn fresh mozzarella

1. Preheat the oven to 350°F (180°C). Spray a 9 × 13-inch (23 × 33 cm) baking dish with nonstick cooking spray.

2. Cut the eggplants in half lengthwise. Using a spoon, scoop out the flesh from the halves, leaving a ½-inch-thick (13 mm) border to create a boat. Roughly chop the scooped-out eggplant and set aside.

3. Place the eggplant boats, cut side up, in the prepared baking dish and transfer to the oven. Bake until the boats are tender yet still hold their shape, about 45 minutes. Remove the boats and leave the oven on.

4. Meanwhile, make the filling. Add the farro to a large pot of salted water and bring to a boil. Reduce the heat to medium-low and simmer until tender, 25 to 30 minutes. Drain and set aside.

5. Heat 1 tablespoon (15 ml) of the olive oil in a large skillet over medium-high heat. Add the reserved chopped eggplant and cook and stir until golden brown and tender, about 10 minutes. Transfer to a bowl and set aside.

continued

6. Reduce the heat to medium. In the same skillet, add the remaining 1 tablespoon (15 ml) olive oil. Add the celery and onion, and cook, stirring occasionally, until soft, 5 to 6 minutes.

7. Add the olives and capers, and cook and stir for 2 minutes. Add the tomato paste and cook and stir until the paste has caramelized, about 2 minutes more. Add the vinegar and sugar, and cook and stir until the sugar dissolves and the vinegar is almost completely evaporated, 2 to 3 minutes more.

8. Add the cooked eggplant and drained farro to the skillet and stir to incorporate. Stir in the almonds, basil, salt, and pepper until combined.

9. Spoon the caponata into the 4 boats and top with the torn mozzarella.

10. Increase the oven temperature to 425°F (220°C). Transfer the baking dish back to the oven and bake until the mozzarella is melted and bubbly, about 10 minutes.

Quinoa, Mushroom, Spinach, and Tomato-Stuffed Eggplant Boats with Turmeric Tahini

~~~~~~~~~~~~~~~~~~~~~~~~~~~~~~~~~~~~

PREP TIME: 20 minutes
COOK TIME: 30 minutes
YIELD: serves 4 as a side dish

Ingredients
BOATS
2 medium eggplants

FILLING
2 tablespoons (30 ml) olive oil
½ cup (85 g) thinly sliced shallots
8 ounces (227 g) thinly sliced cremini
   mushrooms
6 canned Roma tomatoes, drained
   and chopped
1 tablespoon (15 ml) canned
   tomato juice
4 cloves garlic, minced
4 cups (80 g) baby spinach
1 cup (185 g) cooked quinoa
1 teaspoon ground cumin
¼ cup (15 g) chopped cilantro
½ teaspoon sea salt
½ teaspoon freshly ground
   black pepper

SAUCE
¼ cup (60 g) tahini
2 tablespoons (30 ml) apple cider
   vinegar
2 tablespoons (30 ml) water
1 tablespoon (15 ml) ground turmeric
½ teaspoon sea salt

1. Preheat the oven to 425°F (220°C). Line a baking sheet with parchment paper.

2. **To prepare the boats:** Cut the eggplants in half lengthwise. Using a spoon, scoop out the flesh from the halves, leaving a ½-inch-thick (13 mm) border to create a boat. Save the scooped-out eggplant flesh for another use.

3. Place the hollowed-out eggplant boats, cut side up, on the prepared baking sheet, transfer to the oven, and bake for 20 minutes. Set aside.

4. **To make the filling:** Heat the olive oil in a large skillet over medium heat. Add the shallots and mushrooms, and cook, stirring occasionally, for 5 minutes.

5. Add the tomatoes, tomato juice, and garlic and cook for 3 minutes more.

6. Add the baby spinach and cook, stirring occasionally, until wilted, 2 to 3 minutes. Stir in the quinoa, cumin, cilantro, salt, and pepper.

7. Divide the quinoa mixture among the 4 boats. Transfer the filled boats to the oven and bake for 10 minutes, or until lightly browned and bubbly.

8. **To make the sauce:** While the filled boats are baking, make the sauce. In a blender, puree the tahini, vinegar, water, turmeric, and salt until smooth.

9. To serve, drizzle the hot eggplant boats with the sauce. Serve immediately.

Lamb Gyro-Stuffed Eggplant Boats

PREP TIME: 30 minutes
COOK TIME: 40 minutes
YIELD: serves 4 as a main course

Ingredients

BOATS

2 large eggplants
⅓ cup (80 ml) extra-virgin
    olive oil, plus more for brushing
¼ cup (60 g) tahini
2 cloves garlic, minced
2 tablespoons (8 g) fresh parsley
¾ teaspoon sea salt
½ teaspoon ground cumin

FILLING

1 pound (454 g) ground lamb
2 tablespoons (8 g) chopped
    fresh oregano
1 tablespoon (15 ml) hot sauce
1 tablespoon (15 ml) cold water
1 clove garlic, minced
2 teaspoons salt
½ teaspoon freshly ground
    black pepper
1 tablespoon (15 ml) olive oil

SAUCE

1 cup (230 g) nonfat Greek yogurt
1 clove garlic, minced
2 teaspoons freshly squeezed
    lemon juice
1 tablespoon (4 g) chopped fresh
    parsley
1 tablespoon (6 g) chopped fresh mint
½ teaspoon salt

SALAD

2 cups (300 g) halved grape tomatoes
2 cups (200 g) seeded and thinly
    sliced English cucumber
½ cup (58 g) thinly sliced red onion
2 tablespoons (30 ml) extra-virgin
    olive oil
1 tablespoon (15 ml) red wine vinegar
½ teaspoon sea salt
¼ teaspoon freshly ground
    black pepper

1. Preheat the oven to 450°F (230°C). Line a baking sheet with parchment paper.

2. **To prepare the boats:** Cut the eggplants in half lengthwise. Brush the eggplants with a little of the olive oil and place them, cut side down, on the prepared baking sheet.

3. Transfer the baking sheet to the oven and bake until tender, 35 to 40 minutes. Flip the eggplants over and scoop out the flesh with a spoon, creating an eggplant boat. Set the boats aside.

4. Transfer the eggplant flesh, ⅓ cup (80 ml) olive oil, tahini, garlic, parsley, salt, and cumin to the bowl of a food processor. Pulse 4 to 5 times, or until chopped but still chunky. Set aside.

5. **To make the filling:** In a large bowl, combine the ground lamb, oregano, hot sauce, cold water, garlic, salt, and pepper. Knead until the mixture comes together, about 1 minute.

6. Heat a large cast-iron skillet over medium-high heat. Add the olive oil, followed by the meat mixture. Press it into a flat patty. Allow to cook until browned and crispy, 5 to 7 minutes. Start breaking the meat apart into bite-size pieces and then flip the pieces and cook until the other side is browned and crispy and cooked through, another 5 minutes. Transfer the meat to a paper towel–lined plate and keep warm.

7. **To make the sauce:** In a medium bowl, combine the yogurt, garlic, lemon juice, parsley, mint, and salt. Set aside.

8. **To make the salad:** In a large bowl, combine the tomatoes, cucumbers, onion, olive oil, vinegar, salt, and pepper.

9. To assemble the boats, place the eggplant boats on a platter, divide the seasoned eggplant among the 4 boats, and top with the gyro meat and tomato-cucumber salad. Drizzle with the yogurt sauce. Serve immediately.

Roasted Eggplant Boats with Soba Noodles and Mango Salad

PREP TIME: 50 minutes
COOK TIME: 45 minutes
YIELD: serves 4 as a main course

Ingredients
Nonstick cooking spray

BOATS
2 large eggplants

DRESSING
¼ cup (60 ml) seasoned rice
   wine vinegar
1 tablespoon (20 g) honey
½ teaspoon sea salt
3 cloves garlic, minced
1 red chile, seeded and minced
1 tablespoon (15 ml) toasted
   sesame oil
1 tablespoon (6 g) lime zest
2 tablespoons (30 ml) freshly
   squeezed lime juice

FILLING
1 package (14 ounces, or 397 g)
   extra-firm tofu, drained (see
   Note, below)
½ cup (120 ml) coconut oil,
   divided
1 package (9.5 ounces, or 269 g)
   soba noodles
1½ cups (263 g) peeled and diced
   ripe mango
½ cup (30 g) thinly sliced
   Thai basil
½ cup (30 g) chopped cilantro
¼ cup (35 g) chopped peanuts,
   toasted, for garnish

*Note: You can substitute two
8-ounce (227 g) cooked chicken
breasts, chopped, or 12 ounces
(340 g) cooked shrimp, chopped.
Add in the cooked chicken or
shrimp in step 9.*

continued

1. Preheat the oven to 350°F (180°C). Spray a 9 × 13-inch (23 × 33 cm) baking dish with nonstick cooking spray.

2. **To prepare the boats:** Cut the eggplants in half lengthwise. Using a spoon, scoop out the flesh of the halved eggplants, leaving a ½-inch-thick (13 mm) border to create a boat. Roughly chop the scooped-out eggplant and set aside.

3. Place the hollowed-out eggplant boats, cut side up, in the prepared baking dish, and transfer to the preheated oven. Bake until the boats are tender yet still hold their shape, about 45 minutes.

4. **To make the dressing:** Combine the vinegar, honey, and salt in a small saucepan over medium-high heat. Stir until the honey dissolves, about 1 minute. Remove from the heat and stir in the garlic, chile, sesame oil, lime zest, and lime juice. Set aside.

5. **To make the filling:** Wrap the drained tofu in a clean kitchen towel and place a cutting board on top of it. Weight down the cutting board with a heavy pan or books and allow to sit for 30 minutes. Once the water is removed, unwrap the tofu and cut it into ½-inch (13 mm) dice.

6. Heat ¼ cup (60 ml) of the coconut oil in a large skillet over medium-high heat. Add the reserved chopped eggplant and cook, stirring occasionally, until browned and crispy, 8 to 10 minutes. Transfer to a paper towel–lined plate to drain.

7. In the same skillet, heat the remaining ¼ cup (60 ml) coconut oil. Add the tofu and cook, stirring occasionally, until the tofu is browned and crispy on all sides, 8 to 10 minutes. Transfer to a paper towel–lined plate to drain.

8. Bring a large pot of salted water to a boil over high heat. Add the soba noodles. Cook, stirring occasionally, until al dente, 5 to 8 minutes. Drain and rinse under cold water. Transfer to a paper towel–lined plate to drain completely.

9. To assemble the salad, in a large mixing bowl, add the drained soba noodles and pour the dressing over the top. Mix in the eggplant, tofu, mango, basil, and cilantro, and stir to combine.

10. Divide the mixture among the 4 boats and top with the chopped peanuts.

Creamed Corn Eggplant Boats

PREP TIME: 30 minutes
COOK TIME: 55 minutes
YIELD: serves 4 as a side dish

Ingredients
Nonstick cooking spray

BOATS
2 medium eggplants

SAUCE
¼ cup (60 ml) olive oil
2 teaspoons tomato paste
2 cloves garlic, minced
¼ cup (60 ml) dry white wine
1 cup (235 ml) canned chopped
   tomatoes
½ teaspoon sea salt
½ teaspoon freshly ground
   black pepper
½ cup (30 g) thinly sliced
   fresh basil leaves

FILLING
1 tablespoon (15 g) unsalted
   butter
2 teaspoons olive oil
1 cup (160 g) diced sweet onion
2 cloves garlic, minced
1 package (16 ounces, or 455 g)
   frozen corn, thawed
½ cup (120 ml) almond or
   cashew milk
½ teaspoon sea salt
½ teaspoon freshly ground
   black pepper
½ cup (75 g) crumbled queso
   fresco or feta

continued

1. Preheat the oven to 350°F (180°C). Spray a 9 × 13-inch (23 × 33 cm) baking dish with nonstick cooking spray.

2. **To prepare the boats:** Cut the eggplants in half lengthwise. Using a spoon, scoop out the flesh of the halved eggplants, leaving about a ½-inch-thick (13 mm) border to create a boat. Roughly chop the scooped-out eggplant and set aside.

3. Place the hollowed-out eggplant boats, cut side up, in the prepared baking dish, and transfer to the oven. Bake until the boats are tender yet still hold their shape, about 45 minutes. Increase the oven temperature to 450°F (230°C).

4. **To make the sauce:** Heat the olive oil in a large skillet over medium heat. Add the reserved eggplant and cook, stirring occasionally, until golden brown and tender, about 15 minutes. Transfer the eggplant to a paper towel–lined plate to drain excess oil, if any.

5. Return the eggplant to the skillet along with the tomato paste. Cook and stir for 2 minutes. Add the garlic, white wine, and chopped tomatoes. Cook and stir until thickened, 8 to 10 minutes more. Stir in the salt, pepper, and basil, and keep the sauce warm.

6. **To make the filling:** Heat the butter and olive oil in a separate large skillet over medium heat. Add the onion and garlic, and cook and stir until slightly caramelized, 3 to 4 minutes.

7. Add the corn and cook and stir until lightly browned, 3 to 5 minutes.

8. Transfer the mixture to the bowl of a food processor or a blender, along with the almond milk, salt, and pepper. Pulse about 7 to 10 times, or until well combined and finely chopped.

9. To assemble the boats, place the eggplant halves back in the baking dish. Divide the creamed corn among the 4 boats. Top with the eggplant sauce and the crumbled queso fresco. Transfer to the oven and bake until the boats are warmed through and the cheese is slightly browned, 8 to 9 minutes.

Sweet Potato Boats

Asian Stir-Fry–Stuffed Sweet Potatoes

PREP TIME: 20 minutes
COOK TIME: 50 minutes
YIELD: serves 3 as a main course or 6 as a side dish

Ingredients

3 large Japanese or white sweet
   potatoes
2 tablespoons (30 ml) toasted
   sesame oil
¼ cup (40 g) roughly chopped
   red onion
½ cup (75 g) sliced red bell pepper
   (½-inch × 1-inch, or 13-mm ×
   25-mm, pieces)
1 tablespoon (10 g) minced garlic
1½ cups (105 g) broccoli florets
1 cup (70 g) sliced white mushrooms
½ cup (60 g) julienned carrots
Salt and pepper, to taste
Toasted sesame seeds, for garnish

1. Preheat the oven to 425°F (220°C).

2. Pierce the sweet potatoes all over with a fork. Individually wrap them in aluminum foil and bake for 40 to 50 minutes, until fully cooked. Set aside to cool.

3. Meanwhile, heat the toasted sesame oil in large skillet over medium-high heat. Add the onion, bell pepper, and garlic, and cook until fragrant, about 1½ minutes.

4. Add the broccoli, mushrooms, carrots, and and salt and pepper. Continue to cook and stir until the veggies are tender, 3 to 5 minutes, depending on your preference. Remove from the heat and set aside.

5. Slice each potato in half lengthwise and place side by side on a large platter. Gently mash each potato half and push the insides toward the edges, making space for the veggie filling. Use a spoon to add heaping amounts of filling to the 6 boats. Garnish with sesame seeds.

Sweet Potato Boats with Chickpeas and Spinach

PREP TIME: 15 minutes
COOK TIME: 1 hour 15 minutes
YIELD: serves 4 as a main course

Ingredients

4 medium sweet potatoes
1 tablespoon (15 ml) coconut oil
1 cup (160 g) diced sweet onion
2 cloves garlic, minced
1½ tablespoons (23 ml) garam masala
1 teaspoon ground turmeric
¼ teaspoon cayenne
1 pound (454 g) baby spinach, washed
1 can (15.5 ounces, or 439 g) chickpeas, drained and rinsed
1 cup (225 g) cubed paneer (½-inch, or 13-mm, cubes)
Salt and pepper, to taste

1. Preheat the oven to 425°F (220°C). Line a baking sheet with parchment paper.

2. Pierce the sweet potatoes all over with a fork, then place them on the prepared baking sheet. Transfer the sweet potatoes to the oven and cook until a knife inserted into the center comes out easily, 45 minutes to 1 hour. Allow to cool slightly. Once cool, slice the potatoes in half lengthwise and scoop out most of the flesh, leaving a small rim of flesh around the skin. Reserve the flesh. Leave the oven on.

3. While the potatoes are cooking, make the filling. Heat the coconut oil in a large skillet over medium heat. Add the onion and cook, stirring occasionally, until wilted and starting to brown, 4 to 5 minutes. Add the garlic and stir until fragrant, about 30 seconds.

4. Add the garam masala, turmeric, and cayenne, and stir until fragrant, about 30 seconds more.

5. Add the spinach and reserved sweet potato flesh, and cook, stirring occasionally, until the spinach is wilted and well combined, 3 to 5 minutes.

6. Remove from the heat, stir in the chickpeas and paneer, and season with salt and pepper.

7. On the same baking sheet, arrange the 8 boats and fill with the spinach mixture. Transfer back to the oven and bake for another 15 minutes, until lightly browned and bubbly.

Guacamole-Stuffed Sweet Potatoes

PREP TIME: 25 minutes
COOK TIME: 50 minutes
YIELD: serves 3 as a main course or 6 as a side dish

Ingredients

3 large sweet potatoes

1 ripe avocado

1 clove garlic, finely chopped

Juice of ½ lime

½ cup (30 g) roughly chopped
  cilantro, divided

Salt and pepper, to taste

1 can (15.5 ounces, or 439 g)
  chickpeas, drained and rinsed

Nonstick cooking spray

1 tablespoon (15 ml) chili powder

10 cherry tomatoes, quartered

¼ cup (40 g) finely chopped
  red onion

1. Preheat the oven to 425°F (220°C). Line a baking sheet with parchment paper.

2. Pierce the sweet potatoes all over with a fork. Individually wrap them in aluminum foil and bake until fully cooked, 40 to 50 minutes. Set aside to cool. Leave the oven on.

3. Meanwhile, make the guacamole and roast the chickpeas. Peel the avocado and remove the pit. Add the avocado flesh to a small bowl along with the garlic, lime juice, and ¼ cup (15 g) of the cilantro. (The other half will be used for garnish.) Mash all the ingredients together as chunky or smooth as you like. Season with salt and pepper and set aside.

4. Spread the chickpeas on the prepared baking sheet. Spray them with nonstick cooking spray and sprinkle with the chili powder and a little salt. Toss to coat and bake for 20 to 25 minutes.

5. Slice each potato in half lengthwise and place side by side on a large platter. To create a space for the filling, gently mash each half of the potato and push the insides toward the edges, making space for the guacamole.

6. Divide the guacamole among the 6 boats. Top with the chickpeas, tomatoes, red onion, and remaining ¼ cup (15 g) cilantro.

Mediterranean Chickpea–Stuffed Sweet Potatoes

PREP TIME: 20 minutes
COOK TIME: 50 minutes
YIELD: serves 6 as a starter

Ingredients

3 large sweet potatoes

1 can (15.5 ounces, or 439 g) chickpeas, drained and rinsed

1 plum tomato, diced

¼ cup (45 g) finely chopped green bell pepper

¼ cup (25 g) sliced black olives

2 tablespoons (20 g) finely chopped red onion

3 tablespoons (45 ml) extra-virgin olive oil

2 tablespoons (30 ml) red wine vinegar

1 teaspoon dried oregano

Salt and pepper, to taste

½ cup (75 g) crumbled feta cheese

1. Preheat the oven to 425°F (220°C).

2. Pierce the sweet potatoes all over with a fork. Individually wrap them in aluminum foil and bake until fully cooked, 40 to 50 minutes. Set aside to cool.

3. Meanwhile, in a medium bowl, combine the chickpeas, tomato, bell pepper, olives, and onion. Add the olive oil, vinegar, oregano, and salt and pepper, and toss to coat. Mix in the feta cheese.

4. Slice each potato in half lengthwise and place side by side on a large platter. Gently mash each potato half and push the insides toward the edges, making space for the chickpea mixture. Use a spoon to add a heaping amount of chickpea filling to the 6 boats.

S'more-Stuffed Sweet Potatoes

PREP TIME: 30 minutes
COOK TIME: 1 hour
YIELD: serves 2 to 4 as a dessert

Ingredients
2 large sweet potatoes
2 tablespoons (30 ml) extra-virgin
    coconut oil or coconut oil spray,
    for brushing
Ground cinnamon, for sprinkling
1 dark or milk chocolate bar
    (2.8 to 3.0 ounces, or 79 to
    85 g), roughly chopped
1 cup (50 g) mini marshmallows
1 cup (100 g) crushed graham
    crackers

1. Preheat the oven to 425°F (220°C).

2. Pierce the sweet potatoes all over with a fork and brush them with the coconut oil. Bake the potatoes for 40 to 50 minutes. Once the potatoes are cooked, let them cool for 15 to 20 minutes. Leave the oven on.

3. Place the potatoes on a baking sheet and slice in half lengthwise. Mash the insides of each half, carefully keeping it in the skin. Dig a 2-inch (5 cm) space in the center for the filling. Sprinkle some cinnamon over the top.

4. Set the oven to broil. Fill the centers of the 4 boats with the chocolate and top with the marshmallows. Broil until the chocolate starts to melt and the marshmallows are toasty brown, 6 to 8 minutes. Remove from the oven and top with the crushed graham crackers.

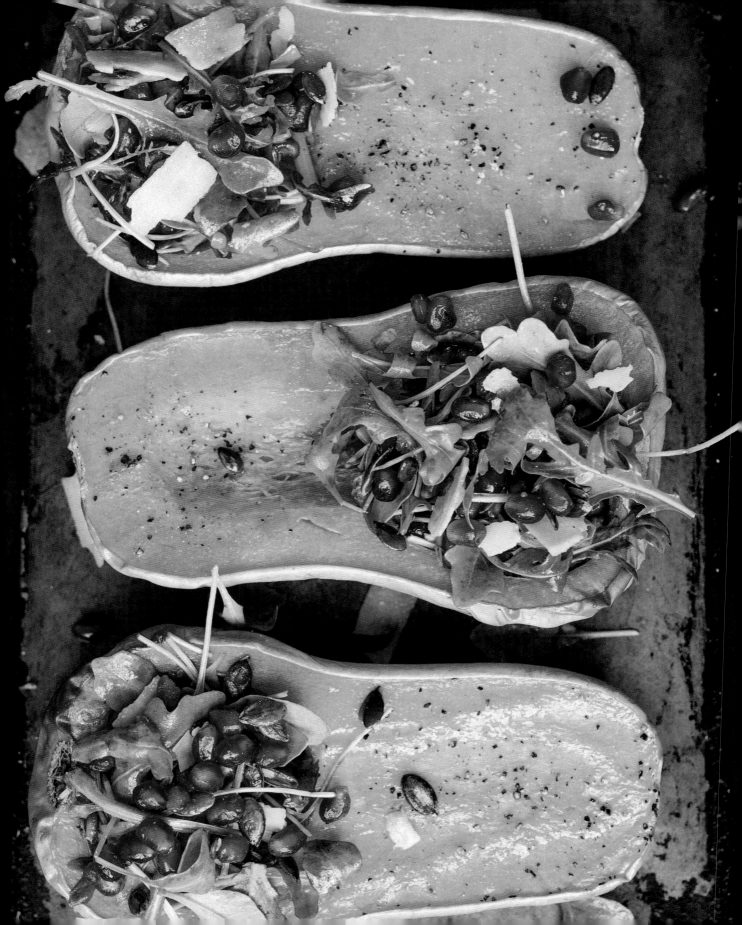

Squash Boats

Roasted Shrimp and Pesto Spaghetti
Squash Boats   66

Maple Acorn Squash Oatmeal Boats   68

Spaghetti Squash Boats with
Chicken Sausage and Peppers   69

Harvest Autumn Acorn Squash
Quinoa Boats   70

Spaghetti Squash Egg Bakes   73

Roasted Butternut Squash Salad Boats   74

Roasted Butternut Squash Boats with
Red Onion, Dried Cranberries, and Tahini   76

Bulgur and Chickpea-Stuffed
Delicata Squash Boats   79

Creole Shrimp and Crab-Stuffed
Chayote Boats   81

Roasted Shrimp and Pesto Spaghetti Squash Boats

PREP TIME: 30 minutes
COOK TIME: 50 minutes
YIELD: serves 4 as a main course

Ingredients
2 medium spaghetti squash
1 pound (454 g) jumbo shrimp,
    peeled and deveined, tails
    left on
Salt and pepper, to taste
½ cup (120 ml) extra-virgin olive
    oil, plus more for brushing and
    tossing
2 cups (120 g) fresh basil leaves
½ cup (50 g) grated Parmesan
    cheese
1½ cups (205 g) pine nuts, divided
1 tablespoon (9 g) chopped garlic
Handful fresh parsley, finely
    chopped, for garnish

*Note: You can save time by using
store-bought pesto, if you prefer.*

1. Preheat the oven to 425°F (220°C). Line 2 baking sheets with parchment paper.

2. Cut the butternut squash in half lengthwise, and with a metal spoon, scrape out the seeds from the center of each side of the squash and discard.

3. Place the squash, cut side down, onto one of the prepared baking sheets and bake until the edges are lightly browned, about 50 minutes. Remove from the oven and let cool for about 15 minutes.

4. Meanwhile, on the second baking sheet, arrange the shrimp 1 inch (2.5 cm) apart. Season with pepper and toss with olive oil. Bake until pink, about 15 minutes. While the squash and shrimp cook, make the pesto.

5. In a food processor, gently pulse together the basil, Parmesan cheese, 1 cup (135 g) of the pine nuts, and garlic, while adding the ½ cup (120 ml) olive oil, a little at a time, until fully combined. Scrape the sides of the bowl if necessary for an even consistency. Season with salt and pepper and transfer to a bowl.

6. Heat a small skillet over medium-high heat, add the remaining ½ cup (70 g) pine nuts, tossing frequently, until light brown, 3 to 4 minutes. Transfer to small dish and set aside.

7. With a fork, gently pull apart the cooled spaghetti squash, keeping the noodles inside the squash boats.

8. Arrange the 4 boats on a serving platter. Pour some of the pesto over the top of each boat. Place the cooked shrimp on top and garnish with the toasted pine nuts and chopped parsley.

Maple Acorn Squash Oatmeal Boats

PREP TIME: 20 minutes
COOK TIME: 45 minutes
YIELD: serves 4 as a breakfast

Ingredients
SQUASH
2 large green acorn squash
2 tablespoons (30 ml) olive oil
2 tablespoons (30 ml) real maple
 syrup
2 tablespoons (18 g) unpacked
 light brown sugar

OATMEAL
2½ cups (590 ml) water
1 cup (80 g) rolled oats
1 teaspoon chia seeds
1 teaspoon flax seeds
¼ cup (41 g) raisins
½ teaspoon ground cinnamon
2 tablespoons (30 ml) maple syrup
½ cup (120 ml) unsweetened
 almond milk, plus more
 as needed
½ cup (50 g) shelled pecans,
 for topping
¼ cup (44 g) dried cranberries,
 for topping
¼ cup (56 g) shelled pumpkin
 seeds, for topping

1. Preheat the oven to 400°F (200°C). Line a baking sheet with parchment paper.

2. **To make the squash:** Cut the butternut squash in half lengthwise, and with a metal spoon, scrape out the seeds from the center of each side of the squash and discard.

3. In a small bowl, combine the olive oil, maple syrup, and brown sugar until smooth. Brush the insides of each half with a generous amount of the maple mixture. Place the squash, flesh side up, on the prepared baking sheet and bake until the edges are lightly browned, 40 to 45 minutes. Set aside.

4. **To make the oatmeal:** In a large saucepan, bring the water to a boil. Add the oats and lower the heat to simmer. Let simmer for 2 to 3 minutes, then stir in the chia seeds, flax seeds, raisins, cinnamon, and maple syrup. Continue to simmer until the oats are tender and the liquid is absorbed, 3 to 5 minutes. Stir in the almond milk, and add more if the oat mixture is too thick. Remove from the heat.

5. Generously fill the 4 boats with the oatmeal. Top with the pecans, dried cranberries, and pumpkin seeds.

Spaghetti Squash Boats with Chicken Sausage and Peppers

PREP TIME: 25 minutes
COOK TIME: 50 minutes
YIELD: serves 2 as a main course

Ingredients

1 medium spaghetti squash

2 tablespoons (30 ml) olive oil, plus more for brushing

Salt and pepper, to taste

3 links (84 g each) organic nitrate-free chicken sausage

1 large green bell pepper, sliced 1½ inches (4 cm) thick

1 medium yellow onion, chopped into 1-inch (2.5 cm) pieces

1 can (15 ounces, or 425 g) tomato sauce

1 cup (115 g) shredded mozzarella (optional)

1. Preheat the oven to 425°F (220°C). Line a baking sheet with parchment paper.

2. Cut the butternut squash in half lengthwise, and with a metal spoon, scrape out the seeds from the center of each side of the squash and discard.

3. Brush the inside of each half with olive oil and season with salt. Place the squash, cut side down, onto the prepared baking sheet and bake for 50 minutes, until the edges are lightly browned. Remove from the oven and let cool for about 15 minutes. Set the oven to broil.

4. While the squash cooks, make the sausage and peppers. Heat a small skillet over medium heat. Cook the sausage on each side until golden and cooked throughout. Set aside to cool. In the same skillet, heat the 2 tablespoons (30 ml) olive oil. Add the peppers and onions, and season with salt and pepper. Cook, tossing occasionally, until the veggies become tender and start to caramelize.

5. Slice the chicken sausages in half lengthwise and then into ½-inch (13 mm) moons. Stir into the pepper mixture.

6. Once the spaghetti squash is cool, use a fork to gently pull apart the spaghetti squash inside each half, keeping the noodles inside the squash boats.

7. Spoon as much of the tomato sauce onto each half as you like. Divide the sausage and peppers between the 2 boats. If using, top with the mozzarella cheese and broil until the cheese is melted and heated through, 5 to 8 minutes. Remove from the oven and serve.

Harvest Autumn Acorn Squash Quinoa Boats

PREP TIME: 20 minutes
COOK TIME: 45 minutes
YIELD: serves 4 as a side dish

Ingredients

2 large green acorn squash
4 to 6 tablespoons (60 to 90 ml)
    extra-virgin olive oil, divided,
    plus more for brushing
Salt and pepper, to taste
2½ cups (590 ml) vegetable broth
    (or an equal amount of water and
    2 veggie bouillon cubes)
1 cup (130 g) quinoa
2 cups (170 g) finely chopped kale
½ cup (75 g) dried cranberries
½ cup (50 g) chopped pecans
Handful fresh parsley, roughly
    chopped
2 sprigs fresh sage, finely chopped
2 tablespoons (30 ml) apple
    cider vinegar

1. Preheat the oven to 400°F (200°C). Line a baking sheet with parchment paper.

2. Cut the butternut squash in half lengthwise, and with a metal spoon, scrape out the seeds from the center of each side of the squash and discard.

3. Brush the insides with 1 to 2 tablespoons (15 to 30 ml) of the olive oil and season with salt. Place the squash, cut side down, on the prepared baking sheet and bake until the edges are lightly browned, 40 to 45 minutes.

4. While the squash is cooking, prepare the quinoa. Bring the vegetable broth to a boil. Add the quinoa, lower the heat, and simmer until the broth is absorbed and the quinoa is tender, about 20 minutes. Remove from heat, transfer to a large bowl, and cool.

5. While the squash and quinoa cook, heat 1 tablespoon (15 ml) of the olive oil in medium skillet. Add the kale and cook and stir until tender, 3 to 4 minutes.

6. Once the quinoa has cooled, add the cooked kale, cranberries, pecans, parsley, sage, remaining 2 to 3 tablespoons (30 to 45 ml) olive oil, and vinegar, and toss until combined. Season with salt and pepper.

7. Scoop heaping amounts of the quinoa mixture into the 4 boats.

Spaghetti Squash Egg Bakes

PREP TIME: 25 minutes
COOK TIME: 1 hour 5 minutes
YIELD: serves 2 as a main course

Ingredients
1 medium spaghetti squash
Olive oil, for brushing
Salt and pepper, to taste
1 ripe avocado
2 large eggs
10 cherry tomatoes, halved
5 to 10 Kalamata olives, pitted and
   sliced in half lengthwise
¼ cup (38 g) crumbled feta cheese
Small handful cilantro, roughly
   chopped
Sriracha, for drizzling

1. Preheat the oven to 425°F (220°C). Line a large baking sheet with parchment paper.

2. Cut the butternut squash in half lengthwise, and with a metal spoon, scrape out the seeds from the center of each side of the squash and discard.

3. Brush the inside of each half with olive oil and season with salt. Place each half, cut side down, on the prepared baking sheet and bake for 50 minutes, until the edges are lightly browned. Remove from the oven and let cool for about 15 minutes.

4. When the squash is almost done baking, slice the avocado in half, remove the pit, and peel. Dice the flesh into ½-inch (13 mm) pieces.

5. Use a metal fork to gently pull apart the spaghetti squash, keeping the noodles inside the squash boats.

6. Make a small 2-inch-round (5 cm) cavity no bigger than 1 inch (2.5 cm) deep in each boat and crack an egg in the middle. Place back into the oven and bake until the egg whites are set and the yolk is slightly runny, another 10 to 15 minutes.

7. To serve, top the 2 boats with the avocado, tomatoes, olives, feta, and cilantro. Season with salt and pepper and drizzle with sriracha.

Roasted Butternut Squash Salad Boats

PREP TIME: 20 minutes
COOK TIME: 55 minutes
YIELD: serves 4 as a main-course salad

Ingredients

BOATS

2 medium butternut squash
2 tablespoons (30 ml) olive oil
1 teaspoon sea salt
1 teaspoon freshly ground
    black pepper

SALAD

4 cups (80 g) wild baby arugula
1 cup (90 g) pomegranate arils
½ cup (113 g) roasted and salted
    pumpkin seeds
½ cup (40 g) shaved Parmesan

DRESSING

1 tablespoon (15 g) Dijon mustard
1 tablespoon (20 g) honey
¼ cup (60 ml) balsamic vinegar
½ teaspoon sea salt
½ teaspoon freshly ground
    black pepper
½ cup (120 ml) extra-virgin
    olive oil

1. Preheat the oven to 400°F (200°C). Line a baking sheet with parchment paper.

2. **To prepare the boats:** Cut the butternut squash in half lengthwise, and with a metal spoon, scrape out the seeds from the center of each side of the squash and discard.

3. Arrange the squash, cut side up, on the prepared baking sheet and season each half with the olive oil, salt, and pepper.

4. Transfer to the oven and roast for 45 to 55 minutes, or until the flesh is fork-tender. Allow to cool slightly while you make the salad.

5. **To make the salad:** In a large bowl, combine the arugula, pomegranate arils, pepitas, and Parmesan.

6. **To make the dressing:** In a medium bowl, whisk together the Dijon, honey, vinegar, salt, and pepper. Slowly add in the olive oil, whisking vigorously until the dressing comes together.

7. Arrange the salad in each of the 4 boats and drizzle with the vinaigrette. Make sure to tell everyone to scoop out the squash as they eat the salad!

Roasted Butternut Squash Boats with Red Onion, Dried Cranberries, and Tahini

PREP TIME: 15 minutes
COOK TIME: 45 minutes
YIELD: serves 4 as a salad

Ingredients

BOATS

2 medium butternut squash
2 tablespoons (30 ml) extra-virgin
  olive oil
2 tablespoons (30 ml) za'atar
1 teaspoon sea salt
1 teaspoon freshly ground black
  pepper

FILLING

1 tablespoon (15 ml) olive oil
1 cup (115 g) thinly sliced red onion
2 cloves garlic, minced
15 ounces (425 g) baby spinach
½ cup (75 g) dried cranberries
½ teaspoon sea salt
½ teaspoon freshly ground
  black pepper

SAUCE

½ cup (120 g) tahini
¼ cup (60 ml) freshly squeezed
  lemon juice
¼ cup (60 ml) water
½ teaspoon sea salt
¼ teaspoon cayenne pepper

1. Preheat the oven to 400°F (200°C). Line a baking sheet with parchment paper.

2. **To prepare the boats:** Cut the butternut squash in half lengthwise, and with a metal spoon, scrape out the seeds and discard. Arrange, cut side up, on the prepared baking sheet and season with the olive oil, za'atar, salt, and pepper.

3. Transfer to the oven and roast until the flesh is fork-tender, 45 to 55 minutes.

4. **To make the filling:** While the squash is roasting, make the filling. Heat the olive oil in a large skillet over medium heat. Add the onion and cook, stirring occasionally, until lightly browned, 4 to 5 minutes. Stir in the garlic.

5. Add the spinach and cook and stir until the spinach is wilted and bright green, about 3 minutes. Stir in the dried cranberries and season with the salt and pepper.

6. **To make the sauce:** In a small bowl, whisk together the tahini, lemon juice, water, salt, and cayenne until smooth.

7. To serve, arrange the 4 boats on a platter and top with the spinach mixture. Drizzle with the tahini sauce and serve hot or at room temperature.

Bulgur and Chickpea–Stuffed Delicata Squash Boats

PREP TIME: 30 minutes
COOK TIME: 30 minutes
YIELD: serves 4 as a main course

Ingredients

BOATS

4 delicata squash of equal size
Olive oil, for brushing
Sea salt, to taste

FILLING

2 cups cooked bulgur (see
    Note, below)
1 can (15.5 ounces, or 439 g)
    chickpeas, drained and rinsed
1 cup (130 g) matchstick-cut carrot
1 bunch scallions, green and white
    parts, finely chopped
Handful fresh flat-leaf parsley,
    roughly chopped
Salt and pepper, to taste
½ cup (70 g) pine nuts

*Note: To cook the bulgur, bring
2½ cups (600 ml) water or stock
to a boil, add 1 cup (140 g)
dry bulgur, reduce the heat to
a simmer, and cover, stirring
occasionally, until the liquid is
absorbed, about 20 minutes.*

DRESSING

½ cup (120 ml) fresh squeezed
    orange juice
½ cup (120 ml) extra-virgin
    olive oil
¼ cup (85 g) agave nectar
2 tablespoons (30 ml) apple
    cider vinegar
1 teaspoon salt
½ teaspoon freshly ground
    black pepper

continued

1. Preheat the oven to 400°F (200°C). Line a baking sheet with parchment paper.

2. **To prepare the boats:** Carefully cut off the ends of each delicata squash, then cut in half lengthwise. With a metal spoon, scrape out the seeds and discard. Place the squash, cut side up, on the prepared baking sheet. Brush the halves with the olive oil and season with the sea salt. Bake for 25 to 30 minutes, until the squash is tender. Remove from the oven.

3. **To make the filling:** While the squash cooks, in a medium bowl, add the bulgur, chickpeas, carrot, scallions, and parsley. Combine well. Season with salt and pepper.

4. Heat a small skillet over medium-high heat. Add the pine nuts, tossing constantly, until they start to brown. Remove from heat and mix one-half of the pine nuts into the filling, reserving the remaining one-half for garnish.

5. **To make the dressing:** In a small bowl, combine the orange juice, olive oil, agave nectar, vinegar, salt, and pepper. Combine until fully blended, then pour over the bulgur mixture. Let sit for at least 20 minutes, for the flavors to absorb.

6. Spoon as much of the bulgur mixture as possible into the 8 boats, mounding it over the tops. Garnish with the reserved toasted pine nuts. Serve immediately.

Creole Shrimp and Crab-Stuffed Chayote Boats

PREP TIME: 30 minutes
COOK TIME: 50 minutes
YIELD: serves 4 as a main course

Ingredients
Nonstick cooking spray
2 large chayote squash
2 tablespoons (30 g) unsalted
    butter plus 2 tablespoons
    (30 g) unsalted butter, melted,
    for drizzling, divided
1 tablespoon (15 ml) olive oil
1 cup (150 g) diced green
    bell pepper
1 cup (100 g) finely chopped
    scallions
½ cup (60 g) diced celery
½ cup (80 g) diced sweet onion
3 cloves garlic, minced
1 bay leaf
1 pound (454 g) medium shrimp,
    peeled, deveined, and roughly
    chopped
1 pound (454 g) jumbo lump
    crabmeat, picked over for shells
1 teaspoon sea salt
½ teaspoon freshly ground
    black pepper
¼ teaspoon cayenne pepper
¼ cup (15 g) chopped fresh parsley
1 large egg
1 cup (50 g) panko bread crumbs

1. Preheat the oven to 350°F (180°C). Spray a 9 × 13-inch (23 × 33 cm) baking dish with nonstick cooking spray.

2. Bring a large pot of salted water to a boil. Meanwhile, peel the chayotes and cut them in half lengthwise. Scoop out and discard the seeds. Drop the halves into the boiling water and cook until tender, about 20 minutes. Drain and allow to cool while you make the seafood filling.

3. Meanwhile, heat 2 tablespoons (30 g) of the butter and the olive oil in a large skillet over medium heat. Add the bell pepper, scallions, celery, onion, garlic, and bay leaf. Cook, stirring occasionally, for 7 to 10 minutes.

4. Stir in the chopped shrimp and cook, stirring occasionally, until the shrimp are pink, 3 to 4 minutes.

5. Remove the bay leaf and stir in the crab. Do not break up the lumps.

6. Season with the salt, pepper, cayenne, and parsley, and remove from the heat.

7. Once the chayote are cool enough to handle, scoop out some of the flesh, creating a boat. Chop the chayote flesh and add it to the seafood mixture.

8. In a small bowl, lightly beat the egg and stir it into the seafood mixture along with the bread crumbs.

9. Arrange the 4 boats in the prepared baking dish and spoon the seafood mixture into the squash. Drizzle with the 2 tablespoons (30 g) melted butter and transfer to the oven. Bake until lightly browned and bubbly, 25 to 30 minutes.

Mushroom Boats

Chicken Enchilada Portobello Boats

PREP TIME: 20 minutes
COOK TIME: 40 minutes
YIELD: serves 4 as a main course

Ingredients

8 large portobello mushrooms

1 tablespoon (15 ml) olive oil

1½ cups (173 g) thinly sliced
sweet onion

1 cup (70 g) thinly sliced
cremini mushrooms

2 cups (300 g) shredded cooked
chicken

1 can (4.5 ounces, or 128 g)
green chiles

½ cup (115 g) sour cream

1½ teaspoons ground cumin

1 teaspoon chili powder

Salt and pepper, to taste

1 can (15 ounces, or 425 g)
enchilada sauce, divided

½ cup (58 g) shredded Monterey
Jack cheese

½ cup (58 g) shredded Cheddar
cheese

½ cup (30 g) chopped cilantro,
for garnish

1 avocado, sliced, for garnish

1 lime, quartered, for serving

1. Preheat the oven to 375°F (190°C). Line a large baking sheet with parchment paper.

2. Wipe the portobellos with a damp paper towel and gently scrape out the gills with a spoon. Arrange the mushrooms, cap sides down, on the prepared baking sheet.

3. Heat the olive oil in a large skillet over medium heat. Add the onions and cremini mushrooms, and cook, stirring occasionally, until golden brown and tender, 5 to 7 minutes. Remove from the heat and stir in the cooked chicken, green chiles, sour cream, cumin, and chili powder. Season with salt and pepper. Stir in half of the enchilada sauce.

4. Divide the chicken mixture among the 8 portobellos. Top with the remaining enchilada sauce and sprinkle with the cheeses.

5. Transfer to the oven and cook until browned and bubbly, 25 to 30 minutes.

6. To serve, transfer the 8 boats to a platter, sprinkle with the chopped cilantro and sliced avocado, and squeeze the lime juice on top.

Mushroom Lasagna Portobello Boats

PREP TIME: 15 minutes
COOK TIME: 25 minutes
YIELD: serves 4 as a main course

Ingredients

8 large portobello mushrooms

2 tablespoons (30 ml) olive oil

½ teaspoon sea salt, plus more to taste

½ teaspoon freshly ground black pepper, plus more to taste

2 cups (500 g) fresh ricotta

¼ cup (25 g) grated Parmesan cheese

¼ cup (25 g) grated Pecorino Romano cheese

¼ cup (15 g) thinly sliced fresh basil leaves

2 cloves garlic, minced

1 large egg

¼ teaspoon freshly grated nutmeg

1½ cups (385 g) marinara sauce

1 cup (115 g) shredded fresh mozzarella

1. Preheat the oven to 425°F (220°C). Line a baking sheet with parchment paper.

2. Wipe the mushrooms with a damp paper towel and gently scrape out the gills with a spoon. Brush with the olive oil and season with salt and pepper.

3. Arrange the mushrooms, cap sides down, on the prepared baking sheet, transfer to the oven, and bake for 10 minutes. Remove and let cool. Leave the oven on.

4. Meanwhile, in a large bowl, combine the ricotta, Parmesan, Pecorino, basil, garlic, egg, nutmeg, ½ teaspoon salt, and ½ teaspoon pepper.

5. To assemble, blot the excess moisture from the baked mushrooms. Spoon 1 heaping tablespoon (16 g) marinara onto each mushroom. Divide the ricotta mixture among the 8 boats, on top of the marinara, and then top with the remaining marinara. Sprinkle with the mozzarella.

6. Transfer back to the oven and bake until the cheese is melted and bubbly, 10 to 12 minutes. Serve immediately.

Tabbouleh-Stuffed Mushrooms

PREP TIME: 20 minutes
COOK TIME: 40 minutes
YIELD: serves 4 to 6 as a starter

Ingredients
Salt and pepper, to taste
1 cup (160 g) bulgur wheat
1 cup (135 g) finely chopped
    cucumber
1 cup (180 g) finely chopped tomato
½ cup (50 g) finely chopped
    scallions
⅔ cup (160 ml) freshly squeezed
    lemon juice, plus more as needed
¼ cup (60 ml) extra-virgin olive oil,
    plus more as needed
1 bunch fresh flat-leaf parsley,
    finely chopped
10 to 15 white stuffing mushrooms
Olive oil spray

1. Preheat the oven to 400°F (200°C). Line a baking sheet with parchment paper.

2. In a medium pot, bring 2½ cups (595 ml) salted water to a boil. Add the bulgur, stir, reduce the heat, and simmer until all the water is absorbed, about 25 minutes.

3. In a medium bowl, combine the cooked bulgur, cucumber, tomato, scallions, lemon juice, olive oil, and all but one-quarter of the chopped parsley. Mix well until fully combined. Season with salt and pepper. If desired, add more lemon juice and/or olive oil depending on your preference. Set aside for at least 20 minutes for the flavors to set, tossing occasionally.

4. While the tabbouleh sets, brush the mushrooms to remove any excess dirt. Carefully remove the stems and scrape out the gills with a small spoon to create a cavity. Place the mushrooms 2 inches (5 cm) apart on the prepared baking sheet.

5. Generously fill the 10 to 15 boats with the tabbouleh mixture, mounding it over the tops. Spray each mushroom with olive oil spray. Transfer to the oven and bake until the tops are crusty golden brown, 10 to 12 minutes. Transfer to a serving dish and top with the reserved parsley.

Wild Mushroom and Herb Polenta in a Portobello Boat

PREP TIME: 30 minutes
COOK TIME: 55 minutes
YIELD: serves 4 as a main course or 8 as a side dish

Ingredients

BOATS
8 large portobello mushrooms
2 tablespoons (30 ml) olive oil,
    for brushing
Salt and pepper, to taste

SAUCE
1 tablespoon (15 g) salted butter
1 tablespoon (15 ml) olive oil
½ cup (80 g) chopped sweet onion
2 cloves garlic, minced
1½ pounds (680 g) mixed wild
    mushrooms (such as cremini,
    shiitake, maitake, and
    chanterelle), sliced
4 cups (80 g) Tuscan kale, stems
    removed and roughly chopped
¼ cup (60 ml) dry sherry
½ cup (120 ml) chicken broth
1 tablespoon (3 g) chopped
    fresh thyme
¼ cup (60 ml) heavy cream
1 teaspoon sea salt
1 teaspoon freshly ground
    black pepper

POLENTA
4 cups (940 ml) chicken broth
2 tablespoons (30 g) salted butter
1¼ cups (175 g) stoneground
    yellow cornmeal
½ cup (40 g) grated Pecorino
    Romano cheese
¼ cup (15 g) chopped fresh parsley
¼ cup (15 g) chopped
    fresh basil
1 teaspoon sea salt
1 teaspoon freshly ground
    black pepper
½ cup (50 g) grated Parmesan
    cheese

continued

1. Preheat the oven to 425°F (220°C). Line a baking sheet with parchment paper.

2. **To prepare the boats:** Wipe the portobellos with a damp paper towel and gentle scrape out the gills with a spoon. Brush with 1 tablespoon (15 ml) of the olive oil and season with salt and pepper.

3. Arrange the portobellos, cap sides down, on the prepared baking sheet, transfer to the oven, and bake for 10 minutes. Let cool.

4. **To make the sauce:** Melt the butter and olive oil in a large skillet over medium-high heat. Add the onion and cook, stirring occasionally, for 3 to 5 minutes. Add the garlic and cook 1 minute more.

5. Add the wild mushrooms and cook, stirring occasionally, until browned and tender, 8 to 10 minutes. Stir in the chopped kale and cook and stir until wilted and tender, about 5 minutes more.

6. Stir in the sherry and allow the liquid to evaporate, about 1 minute. Add the chicken broth, thyme, heavy cream, sea salt, and pepper, and cook until thickened and bubbly, 1 to 2 minutes.

7. **To make the polenta:** While the mushroom sauce is cooking, make the polenta. In a large heavy-bottomed saucepan, heat the broth and butter over high heat until boiling. Reduce the heat to medium-low and slowly whisk in the cornmeal until incorporated.

8. Reduce the heat to low and simmer gently, stirring frequently, until the mixture is thick and creamy, 18 to 20 minutes. Stir in the Pecorino, parsley, basil, salt, and pepper.

9. To assemble, divide the polenta among the 8 baked boats, top with the mushroom sauce, and then sprinkle with the Parmesan.

10. Transfer back into the oven and bake until the cheese is melted and bubbly, 5 to 7 minutes.

Mediterranean Quinoa–Stuffed Mushrooms

PREP TIME: 15 minutes
COOK TIME: 20 minutes
YIELD: serves 6 as a starter

Ingredients

2 tablespoons (30 ml) extra-virgin olive oil, divided

½ cup (75 g) finely chopped red bell pepper

¼ cup (40 g) finely chopped red onion

1 tablespoon (9 g) finely chopped garlic

2 cups (370 g) cooked quinoa

2 cups (60 g) spinach leaves, finely chopped

½ cup (75 g) crumbled feta cheese

1 cup (100 g) grated Parmesan cheese

Salt and pepper, to taste

18 to 20 white button or baby bella mushrooms

Nonstick cooking spray

1. Preheat the oven to 400°F (200°C). Line a baking sheet with parchment paper.

2. In a small skillet, heat 1 tablespoon (15 ml) of the olive oil over medium-high heat. Add the bell pepper and onion. Cook, stirring occasionally, for 2 to 3 minutes. Stir in the garlic and cook for 1 to 2 minutes more. Transfer the mixture to a medium bowl.

3. Add the quinoa, spinach, feta, Parmesan cheese, remaining 1 tablespoon (15 ml) olive oil, and salt and pepper, and combine well.

4. Brush the mushrooms to remove any excess dirt. Carefully remove the stems and gently scrape out the gills with a small spoon to create a cavity. Place the mushrooms 2 inches (5 cm) apart on the prepared baking sheet.

5. Generously fill the 18 to 20 boats with the quinoa mixture, mounding it over the tops. Spray each mushroom with nonstick cooking spray and bake until the tops are crusty and golden brown, 10 to 12 minutes.

Parmesan Baked Eggs in Portobello Boats

PREP TIME: 15 minutes
COOK TIME: 15 minutes
YIELD: serves 4 as a main course

Ingredients
4 large portobello mushrooms
Salt and pepper, to taste
4 large eggs
1 cup (100 g) grated Parmesan
    cheese

1. Preheat the oven to 425°F (220°C). Line a baking sheet with parchment paper. Set aside.

2. Wipe the portobellos with a damp paper towel and gently scrape out the gills with a spoon.

3. Arrange the mushrooms, cap sides down, on the prepared baking sheet, sprinkle with salt and pepper, and bake for 5 minutes. Remove from the oven, and leave the oven on.

4. Adjust the mushroom caps so that they are level on the baking sheet, in order to prevent any of the egg from seeping out the sides. (If necessary, place a piece of folded aluminum foil underneath the mushroom cap as a wedge to level it out.)

5. Carefully crack an egg into each of the 4 boats. Place back in the oven for a second time and bake for another 5 to 7 minutes, until the whites begin to firm up.

6. Remove the sheet from the oven (leaving the oven on) and sprinkle a generous amount of Parmesan around the edges of the eggs, which will help absorb some of the cooking juices. Season the mushrooms with salt and pepper.

7. Place back in oven for the third and final time, and bake for another 2 to 3 minutes.

8. Remove from the oven and serve immediately.

Baked Potato Boats

Shepherd's Pie Potato Boats

PREP TIME: 30 minutes
COOK TIME: 1 hour 20 minutes
YIELD: serves 4 as a main course

Ingredients

BOATS

4 large russet potatoes
2 tablespoons (30 ml) olive oil
1 tablespoon (15 ml) flaky sea salt
    plus ½ teaspoon sea salt
½ cup (120 ml) 2% milk
¼ cup (60 g) unsalted butter
½ teaspoon freshly ground
    black pepper
1 large egg yolk

FILLING

2 tablespoons (30 ml) olive oil
1 cup (160 g) diced sweet onion
1 cup (130 g) peeled and diced carrots
2 cloves garlic, minced
1 pound (454 g) ground lamb or beef
1 teaspoon sea salt
½ teaspoon freshly ground
    black pepper
2 tablespoons (30 g) all-purpose flour
1 tablespoon (16 g) tomato paste
1 cup (225 g) chicken broth
2 teaspoons Worcestershire sauce
2 teaspoons chopped fresh rosemary
1 teaspoon chopped fresh thyme
½ cup (68 g) frozen corn kernels
½ cup (75 g) English peas
1 cup (115 g) grated extra-sharp
    Cheddar cheese

1. Preheat the oven to 400°F (200°C). Line a baking sheet with parchment paper.

2. **To prepare the boats:** Pierce the potatoes all over with a fork. Rub them with the olive oil and season with the 1 tablespoon (15 ml) flaky sea salt. Place on the prepared baking sheet and transfer to the oven. Bake until the skin is crisp and a knife inserted into the center comes out easily, about 1 hour. Leave the oven on.

3. Once baked, cut the potatoes in half lengthwise. Scoop out the flesh and place in a large bowl. Add the milk, butter, ½ teaspoon sea salt, and pepper, and mash until smooth. Add the egg yolk and mix until well combined. Set aside.

4. **To make the filling:** While the potatoes are baking, prepare the filling. Heat the olive oil in a large skillet over medium heat. Add the onions, carrots, and garlic, and cook, stirring occasionally, for 5 to 7 minutes.

5. Add the lamb, salt, and pepper, and cook, breaking up the meat as you go, for 3 to 4 minutes. Sprinkle the meat with the flour and stir to combine.

6. Add the tomato paste, chicken broth, Worcestershire, rosemary, and thyme, and stir to combine. Bring to a boil, reduce the heat to low, cover, and simmer for 10 to 12 minutes. The sauce will thicken slightly. Add the corn and peas, and stir to combine.

7. To assemble, arrange the 8 boats back on the baking sheet and fill them with the lamb mixture.

8. Add the potato mixture to a large resealable plastic bag. Cut off a ½-inch (13 mm) corner and pipe the mashed potatoes onto the filled potatoes. Sprinkle with the cheese.

9. Transfer back to the oven and bake until the cheese is melted, browned, and bubbly, 15 to 20 minutes.

Baked Potato Boats with Artichokes, Spinach, and Mozzarella

PREP TIME: 20 minutes
COOK TIME: 1 hour 10 minutes
YIELD: serves 4 as a main course or 8 as a side dish

Ingredients

BOATS

4 large russet potatoes

2 tablespoons (30 ml) olive oil

1 tablespoon (15 ml) flaky sea salt

VEGETABLE FILLING

1 tablespoon (15 ml) olive oil

1 package (8 ounces, or 225 g) frozen artichokes, thawed and roughly chopped

2 pounds (907 g) baby spinach

2 cloves garlic, minced

½ teaspoon sea salt

½ teaspoon freshly ground black pepper

MASHED POTATOES

½ cup (120 ml) 2% milk

2 tablespoons (30 g) unsalted butter

½ teaspoon sea salt

1 teaspoon freshly ground black pepper

1 cup (115 g) shredded mozzarella, for topping

1. Preheat the oven to 400°F (200°C). Line a baking sheet with parchment paper.

2. **To make the boats:** Pierce the potatoes all over with a fork. Rub them with the olive oil and season with the salt. Place on the prepared baking sheet and transfer to the oven. Bake until the skin is crisp and a knife inserted into the center comes out easily, about 1 hour. Leave the oven on.

3. **To make the vegetable filling:** While the potatoes are cooking, make the vegetable filling. Heat the oil in a large skillet over medium heat. Add the thawed artichoke hearts and cook, stirring occasionally, for 3 minutes.

4. Add the baby spinach and cook and stir until the spinach is wilted, 2 minutes more. Stir in the garlic. Season with the salt and pepper. Remove from the heat and set aside.

5. **To make the mashed potatoes:** Once the potatoes are done cooking, cut them in half lengthwise and scoop out the flesh into a large bowl. Mash with the milk, butter, salt, and pepper until smooth and creamy.

6. To assemble, arrange the 8 boats back on the baking sheet and fill with the mashed potatoes. Divide the vegetable filling among the halves and sprinkle with the mozzarella.

7. Transfer back to the oven and bake until the cheese is melted and bubbly, 10 minutes. Serve immediately.

Moussaka-Stuffed Potato Boats

PREP TIME: 30 minutes
COOK TIME: 1 hour 45 minutes
YIELD: serves 4 as a main course or 8 as a side dish

Ingredients

BOATS
4 large russet potatoes
2 tablespoons (30 ml) olive oil
1 tablespoon (15 ml) flaky
    sea salt

MEAT SAUCE
2 tablespoons (30 ml) olive oil
1 cup (115 g) diced sweet onion
1 cup (130 g) peeled and diced
    carrots
2 cloves garlic, minced
1 pound (454 g) ground lamb
½ cup (120 ml) dry white wine
1 tablespoon (15 ml) dried oregano
1 teaspoon ground cinnamon
½ teaspoon ground allspice
1 can (28 ounces, or 793 g) crushed
    tomatoes
¼ cup (15 g) chopped fresh parsley
½ teaspoon sea salt

EGGPLANT FILLING
1 tablespoon (15 ml) olive oil
2 large eggplants, cut into
    ½-inch (13 mm) cubes
½ cup (120 ml) water
1 tablespoon (15 ml)
    lemon juice
1 teaspoon sea salt

YOGURT SAUCE
1 cup (230 g) 2% Greek
    yogurt
2 large eggs
1 cup (150 g) crumbled
    Greek feta
½ teaspoon sea salt

1. Preheat the oven to 400°F (200°C). Line a baking sheet with parchment paper.

2. **To prepare the boats:** Pierce the potatoes all over with a fork. Rub them with the olive oil and season with the flaky sea salt. Place on the prepared baking sheet and transfer to the oven. Bake until the skin is crisp and a knife inserted into the center comes out easily, about 1 hour. Leave the oven on.

3. Once baked, cut the potatoes in half lengthwise. Scoop out the flesh and place into a large bowl, reserving 2 cups (450 g) for the yogurt sauce and the rest for another use.

4. **To make the meat sauce:** While the potatoes are baking, make the meat sauce. Heat the olive oil in a large skillet over medium heat. Add the onion and carrots and cook, stirring occasionally, for 5 to 7 minutes. Stir in the garlic.

5. Add the ground lamb and cook, stirring and breaking up the meat as you go, until the meat is browned, 3 to 5 minutes.

6. Add the wine and cook until the liquid has mostly evaporated, about 2 minutes.

7. Stir in the oregano, cinnamon, and allspice, and cook until fragrant, about 1 minute.

8. Add the crushed tomatoes and stir to combine. Reduce the heat to low and simmer, stirring occasionally, for 45 minutes. Stir in the parsley and salt.

9. **To make the eggplant filling:** While the potatoes and meat sauce are cooking, prepare the eggplant filling. Heat the olive oil in a separate large skillet over medium heat. Add the eggplant, water, lemon juice, and salt, and cook, stirring occasionally, until the eggplant is soft and caramelized, 15 to 20 minutes.

10. **To make the yogurt sauce:** Mash the 2 cups (450 g) of reserved potato until smooth and creamy. Add the yogurt and eggs, and whisk until smooth. Stir in the crumbled feta and salt. The sauce will be very runny.

11. To assemble, arrange the 8 boats back on the baking sheet. Fill with the meat sauce, then the eggplant filling, and top with the yogurt sauce. Don't worry if the yogurt sauce drips down the sides.

12. Transfer back to the oven and bake until the sauce is set, 30 to 45 minutes. Allow to rest for a few minutes before serving.

Buffalo Cauliflower–Stuffed Baked Potatoes

PREP TIME: 20 minutes
COOK TIME: 1 hour 50 minutes
YIELD: serves 4 as a main course or 8 as a side dish

Ingredients

4 large russet potatoes

3 tablespoons (45 ml) olive oil, divided

1 tablespoon (15 ml) flaky sea salt

Nonstick cooking spray

½ cup (64 g) brown rice flour

½ cup (120 ml) water

1 teaspoon garlic powder

½ teaspoon sea salt

½ teaspoon freshly ground black pepper

1 medium cauliflower, cut into bite-size pieces

2 tablespoons (30 g) unsalted butter, melted

⅔ cup (160 ml) Buffalo hot sauce

1 cup (120 g) crumbled blue cheese, for topping

4 scallions, finely chopped, for topping

1. Preheat the oven to 400°F (200°C). Line a baking sheet with parchment.

2. Pierce the potatoes all over with a fork. Rub with 2 tablespoons (30 ml) of the oil and season with the flaky sea salt. Place on the prepared baking sheet and transfer to the oven. Bake until the skin is crisp and a knife inserted in the center comes out easily, about 1 hour. Set aside to cool.

3. After the potatoes are done, make the cauliflower. Increase the oven temperature to 450°F (230°C). Line another baking sheet with parchment, spray it with nonstick cooking spray, and set aside.

4. In a large bowl, whisk together the rice flour, water, garlic powder, sea salt, and pepper. Add the cauliflower and toss to coat.

5. Spread the cauliflower evenly on the prepared baking sheet and cook for 15 minutes, flipping halfway through the cooking time.

6. In a separate large bowl, whisk together the melted butter and Buffalo sauce. Add the cooked cauliflower and toss to coat. Spread the mixture evenly onto the prepared baking sheet and transfer back to the oven. Bake for 20 to 35 minutes, flipping halfway through the cooking time.

7. Once the potatoes are cool enough to handle, cut them in half lengthwise. Scoop out the baked potato, reserving it for another use.

8. To assemble, divide the hot Buffalo cauliflower among the 8 boats, top with the scallions and crumbled blue cheese, and serve immediately.

Baked Potato Boats with Broccoli, Mushrooms, and Bacon

PREP TIME: 15 minutes
COOK TIME: 1 hour 10 minutes
YIELD: serves 4 as a main course or 8 as a side dish

Ingredients

4 large russet potatoes
2 tablespoons (30 ml) olive oil
1 tablespoon (15 ml) flaky sea salt
    plus 1 teaspoon sea salt, divided
4 slices thick-cut bacon
1 pound (454 g) cremini mushrooms,
    sliced
4 cups (280 g) fresh broccoli florets
¼ cup (60 g) unsalted butter
1 teaspoon freshly ground
    black pepper
½ cup (40 g) shredded Parmesan

1. Preheat the oven to 400°F (200°C). Line a baking sheet with parchment paper.

2. Pierce the potatoes all over with a fork. Rub them with the olive oil and season with the 1 tablespoon (15 ml) flaky sea salt. Place on the prepared baking sheet and transfer to the oven. Bake until the skin is crisp and a knife inserted into the center comes out easily, about 1 hour. Leave the oven on.

3. While the potatoes are baking, make the filling. In a large skillet over medium heat, add the bacon and cook, 3 to 5 minutes per side, or to the desired degree of crispness. Transfer the bacon to a paper towel–lined plate to cool slightly.

4. Pour off all but 1 tablespoon (15 ml) of bacon grease from the skillet. Return the skillet to medium heat and add the mushrooms. Cook until browned and tender, stirring occasionally, about 5 minutes.

5. Add the broccoli florets and cook and stir until the broccoli is tender-crisp, 3 to 4 minutes more.

6. Once the potatoes are baked, remove them from the oven and cut in half lengthwise, but do not cut all the way through so that the potato is still connected. Fluff the insides with a fork, adding 1 tablespoon (15 g) of butter per whole potato. Season with the remaining 1 teaspoon salt and the pepper.

7. To assemble, arrange the 4 boats back on the baking sheet. Divide the vegetable mixture among the potatoes. Crumble a slice of bacon onto each potato and sprinkle with the Parmesan.

8. Transfer back to the oven and cook until the cheese is melted and bubbly, about 10 minutes. Serve immediately.

Broccoli and Tahini-Stuffed Potatoes

~~~~~~

PREP TIME: 15 minutes
COOK TIME: 55 minutes
YIELD: serves 4 as a main course or 8 as a side dish

Ingredients
4 medium russet potatoes
2½ cups (175 g) fresh broccoli
    florets
Juice of 1 lemon
Salt and pepper, to taste
1 cup (240 g) tahini, or to taste,
    for topping
Crushed red pepper flakes,
    for topping

*Note: see recipe photo on
page 96.*

1. Preheat the oven to 425°F (220°C). Line a baking sheet with parchment paper.

2. Pierce the potatoes all over with a fork. Individually wrap them in aluminum foil and bake until the potatoes are fully cooked, 40 to 50 minutes. Once cooked, set aside to cool. Leave the oven on.

3. Meanwhile, bring a medium pot of water to a boil. Add the broccoli and boil until just tender, 3 to 4 minutes. Drain and cool. (Be sure not to overcook the broccoli or it will turn into broccoli mash when you chop it.) Finely chop the broccoli, leaving some larger pieces. Toss it with the lemon juice and season with salt and pepper.

4. Once the potatoes are cool enough to handle, cut them in half lengthwise and arrange them back on the baking sheet. Gently spoon out a cavity in each potato half, creating a space for the broccoli.

5. To assemble, divide the broccoli, in heaping amounts, among the 8 boats. Transfer back to the oven and bake for 3 minutes.

6. To serve, spoon as much (or as little) tahini on the top as you like and sprinkle with red pepper flakes.

Avocado Boats

Bacon and Scrambled Egg-Stuffed Avocado Boats

PREP TIME: 15 minutes
COOK TIME: 20 minutes
YIELD: serves 4 as a breakfast

Ingredients

8 slices uncured bacon
6 large eggs
¼ cup (60 ml) whole milk
4 semi-ripe Hass avocados
½ cup (50 g) finely chopped
   scallions, for topping
Sriracha, for topping (optional)

1. Place the bacon on a paper towel–lined microwave-safe plate and cover with more paper towels. Microwave on high until just cooked, 3 to 4 minutes. (If you prefer, you can cook the bacon in a skillet.) Transfer the bacon to a clean paper towel–lined plate to drain and cool. Once the bacon is cool, roughly chop it into small pieces. Set aside.

2. In a medium bowl, beat the eggs and stir in the milk. Heat a large skillet over medium heat. Add the chopped bacon. It should start to sizzle and release some grease. Once it does, add the eggs and scramble with the bacon until the eggs are fully cooked. Remove from the heat and set aside.

3. Slice the avocados in half and remove the pits. With a spoon, scoop out a little bit of the centers, reserving for another use, to make room for the eggs. (Be careful not to remove too much of the delicious flesh!) Divide the egg mixture among the 8 boats.

4. Top with chopped scallions and sriracha (if using).

Avocado Boats with Smoked Salmon and Poached Eggs

PREP TIME: 15 minutes
COOK TIME: 15 minutes
YIELD: serves 4 as a breakfast

Ingredients
4 just-ripe large avocados
8 ounces (227 g) smoked salmon
8 large eggs
Salt and pepper, to taste
2 Roma tomatoes, diced
¼ cup (29 g) thinly sliced
   red onion
1½ tablespoons (14 g) drained and
   rinsed capers

1. Preheat the oven to 425°F (220°C). Line a baking sheet with parchment paper.

2. Slice the avocados in half and remove the pits. If the pit holes look small, scoop out some of the avocado flesh, reserving for another use, so that the space will hold 1 egg.

3. Arrange the avocados on the prepared baking sheet and line the hollows with the smoked salmon.

4. Crack an egg into each avocado boat on top of the salmon. Season with salt and pepper.

5. Carefully transfer the baking sheet to the oven and bake for 10 to 15 minutes, depending on the desired degree of yolk doneness.

6. To serve, transfer to a plate and top the 8 boats with the tomatoes, red onion, and capers.

Chicken BLT-Stuffed Avocados

PREP TIME: 15 minutes
COOK TIME: 30 minutes
YIELD: serves 4 as a main course or 8 as a starter or side dish

Ingredients

1 pound (454 g) boneless,
  skinless chicken breast
  (you can substitute rotisserie
  or already-cooked chicken
  for a quicker alternative)
Garlic powder, to taste
Salt and pepper, to taste
½ cup (120 ml) extra-virgin
  olive oil, plus more for drizzling
10 slices uncured bacon
2 cups (40 g) shredded romaine
  lettuce
1 large tomato, finely chopped
¼ cup (60 ml) red wine or
  balsamic vinegar
4 semi-ripe Hass avocados

1. Preheat the oven to 400°F (200°C). Line a baking sheet with parchment paper.

2. Season both sides of the chicken with garlic powder, salt, pepper, and a drizzle of olive oil. Place the seasoned chicken on the prepared baking sheet, transfer to the oven, and bake, turning once, until the chicken is fully cooked and light golden brown, 25 to 30 minutes. Let cool.

3. Once cooled, dice the chicken into ½-inch (13 mm) pieces and set aside.

4. While the chicken cooks, prepare the bacon. Working in batches, if necessary, place the bacon on a paper towel–lined microwave-safe plate and cover with more paper towels. Microwave on high until crispy, 4 to 5 minutes. (If you prefer, you can cook the bacon in a skillet until crispy.) Transfer the bacon to a clean paper towel–lined plate to drain and cool.

5. In a medium bowl, add the lettuce, tomato, and 1 cup (110 g) of the diced chicken. In a small bowl, combine the ½ cup (120 ml) olive oil and the vinegar. Pour the vinaigrette over the chicken-lettuce mixture and toss to coat. Crumble the bacon and add most of it to the mixture, reserving some for garnish.

6. Slice the avocados in half and remove the pits. With a spoon, scoop out the centers, reserving for another use, to create a larger space for the filling, leaving some flesh around the edges.

7. To assemble, divide the chicken-lettuce mixture among the 8 boats, using a small spoon to pack in as much of the mixture as possible, until it's mounding over the tops. Top with the reserved bacon and season with black pepper.

Southwestern Shrimp and Lobster-Stuffed Avocados

PREP TIME: 20 minutes
COOK TIME: 20 minutes
YIELD: serves 3 as a main course or 6 as a starter or side dish

Ingredients

3 lobster tails (4 ounces, or
   115 g, each)

½ pound (227 g) shrimp, peeled
   and deveined

3 to 4 tablespoons (45 to 60 ml)
   extra-virgin olive oil, plus more
   for drizzling

Salt and pepper, to taste

1 cup (172 g) canned black beans,
   drained and rinsed

1 cup (225 g) canned sweet corn,
   drained and rinsed

¼ cup (40 g) finely chopped
   red onion

Handful fresh cilantro, roughly
   chopped

¼ cup (40 ml) freshly squeezed
   lime juice

3 just-ripe Hass avocados

1. Preheat the oven to 425°F (220°C). Line a baking sheet with parchment paper.

2. Slice each lobster tail down the middle with a sharp knife. Place the lobster tails and the shrimp onto the prepared baking sheet, drizzle with olive oil, and season with salt and pepper. Bake until the seafood is pink and tender, 15 to 18 minutes. Set aside to cool.

3. In a medium bowl, combine the black beans, corn, red onion, and cilantro. Remove the meat from the lobster tail and discard the shell. Chop the lobster and shrimp into ¼-inch (6 mm) pieces, then add to the bowl along with the lime juice, 3 to 4 tablespoons (45 to 60 ml) olive oil, and salt and pepper.

4. Slice the avocados in half and remove the pits. With a spoon, scoop out the centers, reserving for another use, to create a larger space for the filling, leaving some flesh around the edges.

5. To assemble, divide the lobster-shrimp mixture among the 6 boats, using a small spoon to pack the avocados with the mixture, mounding it over the tops.

Curried Egg Salad Avocado Boats

~~~~~~

TOTAL TIME: 20 minutes
YIELD: serves 8 as a starter

Ingredients
¼ cup (60 g) mayonnaise
2 tablespoons (32 g) bottled mango
    chutney
1 tablespoon (15 ml) freshly
    squeezed lemon juice
1 teaspoon Dijon mustard
1 teaspoon sea salt
1 teaspoon curry powder
1 teaspoon hot sauce
½ teaspoon ground cumin
½ teaspoon celery seed
6 large hard-boiled eggs, cooled
    and peeled
½ cup (60 g) finely chopped celery
¼ cup (38 g) finely chopped red
    bell pepper
4 ripe large avocados
2 scallions, finely chopped

1. In a blender, combine the mayonnaise, mango chutney, lemon juice, mustard, salt, curry powder, hot sauce, cumin, and celery seed. Puree until well combined.

2. In a large bowl, chop the eggs with a potato masher or whisk until roughly chopped. Add the sauce mixture and stir to combine.

3. Stir in the celery and bell pepper. Set aside.

4. When ready to serve, slice the avocados in half, remove the pit, and scoop out some of the avocado flesh, reserving for another use. Spoon the egg salad into the 8 boats, top with scallions, and serve with a spoon and crackers to make sure you get a little avocado with every bite!

Crab, Green Mango, and Coconut Salad Avocado Boats

TOTAL TIME: 25 minutes
YIELD: serves 8 as a salad

Ingredients
2 tablespoons (30 ml) sriracha
1 tablespoon (20 g) honey
1 shallot, minced
2 tablespoons (30 ml) fish sauce
½ cup (120 ml) freshly squeezed
    lime juice
¼ cup (60 ml) toasted sesame oil
½ pound (227 g) jumbo lump
    crabmeat, picked over for shells
1 large green mango, peeled
    and julienned
1 large seedless cucumber, seeded
    and julienned
¼ cup (15 g) sliced basil leaves
¼ cup (15 g) sliced mint leaves
¼ cup (15 g) cilantro leaves
¼ cup (25 g) thinly sliced scallions
4 ripe large avocados
¼ cup (18 g) unsweetened flaked
    coconut, toasted

1. In a large bowl, whisk together the sriracha, honey, shallot, fish sauce, lime juice, and sesame oil.

2. Add the crab, mango, cucumber, basil, mint, cilantro, and scallions. Toss to coat in the dressing, being careful not to break up the crabmeat too much.

3. When ready to serve, slice the avocados in half and remove the pits. Scoop out a little of the avocado flesh, reserving for another use, so that you have a nice bowl. Spoon in the crab and mango salad into the 8 boats, and top with the toasted coconut. Serve immediately.

Scallop Ceviche Avocado Boats

TOTAL TIME: 2 to 4 hours
YIELD: serves 8 as a starter

Ingredients
1 pound (454 g) baby scallops
2 green tomatoes, diced
¼ cup (40 g) minced shallot
¼ cup (36 g) seeded and minced
    jalapeño
⅓ cup (80 ml) freshly squeezed
    lime juice
¾ cup (175 ml) orange juice
1½ teaspoons sea salt
4 ripe large avocados
½ cup (30 g) chopped cilantro

1. In a large bowl, combine the baby scallops, green tomatoes, shallot, jalapeño, lime juice, orange juice, and salt. Stir until well combined. Cover and refrigerate for 2 to 4 hours, stirring occasionally.

2. Once the ceviche is marinated, prepare the avocado boats. (When marinated, the scallops will be opaque and firmer in texture.) Slice the avocados in half, remove the pit, and score the flesh, making squares, but not cutting through the skin. Scoop out the diced avocado and add it to the marinated ceviche along with the cilantro. Toss gently to incorporate.

3. Scoop the ceviche back into the avocado boats and serve.

Southwestern-Stuffed Avocado Boats

~~~~~~ 🍴

TOTAL TIME: 15 minutes
YIELD: serves 8 as a side dish or snack

Ingredients

2 cups (345 g) canned black beans,
   drained and rinsed

2 cups (450 g) canned sweet corn,
   drained and rinsed

4 plum tomatoes, diced

¼ cup (40 g) chopped red onion

Handful fresh cilantro, roughly
   chopped

¼ cup (60 ml) freshly squeezed
   lime juice

3 to 4 tablespoons (45 to 60 ml)
   extra-virgin olive oil

Salt and pepper, to taste

4 just-ripe Hass avocados

1. In a medium bowl, combine the black beans, corn, tomatoes, red onion, and cilantro.

2. Add the lime juice and olive oil, and season with salt and pepper.

3. Slice the avocados in half and remove the pits. With a spoon, scoop out the centers, reserving for another use, to create a larger space for the filling, leaving some flesh around the edges.

4. To assemble, divide the filling among the 8 boats, using a small spoon to pack the avocados with the filling, mounding it over the tops.

Tuna Poke Avocado Boats

TOTAL TIME: 50 minutes
YIELD: serves 8 as a starter

Ingredients

1½ pounds (680 g) ahi tuna, sushi grade

½ cup (58 g) thinly sliced sweet onion

3 scallions, chopped

1 teaspoon peeled and grated fresh ginger

3 cloves garlic, minced

½ cup (120 ml) tamari

2 teaspoons toasted sesame oil

½ teaspoon crushed red pepper flakes

1 teaspoon Chinese chili sauce

4 ripe large avocados

1. Cut the tuna into ½-inch (13 mm) cubes. Place in a large glass or nonreactive bowl, cover, and refrigerate.

2. In a medium glass or nonreactive bowl, add the onion, scallions, ginger, garlic, tamari, sesame oil, red pepper flakes, and chili sauce. Combine well and allow to marinate for at least 30 minutes.

3. When ready to serve, slice the avocados in half, remove the pit, and score the flesh, making squares, but not cutting through the skin. Scoop out the diced avocado and add it to the diced tuna. Pour the marinade over the tuna and avocado, and gently toss together.

4. To serve, spoon the poke into the 8 boats and serve with chopsticks.

Grilled Avocado Boats with Shrimp and Pineapple Salsa

~~~~~~~~~~~~~~~~~~~~~~~~~~~~~~~~~~

PREP TIME: 30 minutes
COOK TIME: 10 minutes
YIELD: serves 4 as a starter

Ingredients

SALSA

1 cup (155 g) diced pineapple
1 cup (180 g) seeded and diced tomato
¼ cup (40 g) diced red onion
1 small chile, seeded and diced
¼ cup (60 ml) freshly squeezed
    lime juice
¼ cup (15 g) chopped cilantro
½ teaspoon salt

BOATS

2 large avocados
1 tablespoon (15 ml) coconut oil,
    melted
Juice of 1 lime
Salt and pepper, to taste

SHRIMP

1½ teaspoons paprika
1 teaspoon cayenne
1 teaspoon salt
½ teaspoon onion powder
½ teaspoon garlic powder
½ teaspoon dried oregano
½ teaspoon ground cumin
1 tablespoon (15 ml) hot sauce
2 tablespoons (30 ml) olive oil
1 pound (454 g) medium shrimp,
    peeled and deveined
Skewers, for grilling

1. **To make the salsa:** In a medium bowl, add the pineapple, tomato, red onion, chile, lime juice, cilantro, and salt. Combine well and set aside to allow the flavors to develop.

2. Preheat a grill to medium-high heat. While the grill is heating up, prepare the avocados.

3. **To make the boats:** Cut the avocados in half, remove the pit, and arrange the avocados on a baking sheet. Brush with the coconut oil, drizzle with the lime juice, and season with salt and pepper.

4. **To make the shrimp:** In a separate large bowl, stir together the paprika, cayenne, salt, onion powder, garlic powder, oregano, cumin, hot sauce, and olive oil. Add the shrimp and toss to coat. Place the shrimp on the skewers to grill them.

5. Once the grill is hot, grill the avocado, flesh side down, until you have nice grill marks, 2 to 3 minutes. Set aside.

6. Grill the shrimp until bright pink and no longer translucent, about 3 minutes per side. Remove the shrimp from the skewers and roughly chop.

7. Add the chopped shrimp to the salsa and toss to coat.

8. Spoon the shrimp and salsa mixture into the 4 boats.

Tomato Boats

Greek Lamb and Rice-Stuffed Tomato Boats

PREP TIME: 20 minutes
COOK TIME: 50 minutes
YIELD: serves 4 as a main course or 8 as a side dish

Ingredients
Nonstick cooking spray
¾ pound (340 g) ground lamb
1 tablespoon (15 ml) olive oil
1 cup (160 g) diced sweet onion
3 cloves garlic, minced
2 teaspoons ground cinnamon
1 teaspoon salt
¼ teaspoon cayenne
1 cup (185 g) basmati rice
1 cup (245 g) tomato sauce
1½ cups (355 ml) chicken broth
8 large globe tomatoes
½ cup (75 g) crumbled Greek feta

1. Preheat the oven to 350°F (180°C). Spray a 9 × 13-inch (23 × 33 cm) baking dish with nonstick cooking spray.

2. In a large skillet over medium heat, add the ground lamb. Cook, stirring and breaking up the meat as you go, until no longer pink, 5 to 7 minutes. Drain the excess fat.

3. To the same skillet, add the olive oil, onion, garlic, cinnamon, salt, cayenne, rice, tomato sauce, and broth. Cook, stirring occasionally, until the rice is almost cooked and most of the liquid has been absorbed, about 15 minutes.

4. While the rice is cooking, prepare the tomatoes by slicing a small piece off the bottom of each, making a flat bottom. Cut off the top one-third of each tomato and scoop out the seeds and inside pulp, leaving a stable boat behind. Discard the pulp and seeds. (You can keep or discard the tomato tops.) Arrange the tomatoes in the prepared baking dish.

5. Spoon the almost-cooked rice mixture into the 8 boats, along with any remaining liquid. Sprinkle with the feta cheese. Transfer to the oven and bake until the tomatoes have softened and the rice is cooked, 20 to 25 minutes.

Caprese Salad–Stuffed Tomato Boats

TOTAL TIME: 20 minutes
YIELD: serves 8 as a salad

Ingredients

8 large globe tomatoes

2 pints (600 g) heirloom grape
   tomatoes, halved

1 fresh mozzarella ball (8 ounces,
   or 227 g), diced

½ cup (30 g) thinly sliced fresh
   basil leaves

1 teaspoon sea salt

½ teaspoon freshly ground
   black pepper

2 tablespoons (30 ml) aged
   balsamic vinegar

2 tablespoons (30 ml) extra-virgin
   olive oil

1. Prepare the globe tomatoes by slicing a small piece off the bottom of each, making a flat bottom. Cut ½ inch (13 mm) from the top of each tomato and scoop out the seeds and pulp, leaving a tomato boat. Discard the top, pulp, and seeds.

2. In a large bowl, combine the halved tomatoes, mozzarella, basil, salt, pepper, balsamic vinegar, and olive oil.

3. Spoon the salad into the 8 boats.

Shakshuka Tomato Boats

PREP TIME: 20 minutes
COOK TIME: 40 minutes
YIELD: serves 4 as a main course

Ingredients

Nonstick cooking spray
8 large globe tomatoes
5 tablespoons (75 ml) olive oil,
  divided
1 teaspoon salt, plus more to taste
1 teaspoon freshly ground black
  pepper, plus more to taste
1 cup (115 g) thinly sliced
  sweet onion
1 cup (150 g) thinly sliced red
  bell pepper
4 cloves garlic, minced
1 teaspoon ground cumin
¼ teaspoon ground cayenne
1 can (28 ounces, or 794 g)
  chopped or diced tomatoes
  with their juices
½ cup (30 g) torn fresh basil
  leaves
1 cup (150 g) crumbled sheep's
  milk feta
8 large eggs
Warm pita bread, for serving

1. Preheat the oven to 400°F (200°C). Spray a 9 × 13-inch (23 × 33 cm) baking dish with nonstick cooking spray.

2. Prepare the tomatoes by slicing a small piece off the bottom of each, making a flat bottom. Cut off the top one-third off each tomato and scoop out the seeds and pulp. Discard the top, seeds, and pulp. Arrange in the prepared baking dish. Drizzle with 2 tablespoons (30 ml) of the olive oil and season with salt and pepper. Transfer to the oven and roast until the tomatoes are tender and slightly caramelized, 25 to 30 minutes.

3. While the tomatoes are roasting, make the sauce. In a large, deep skillet over medium heat, heat the remaining 3 tablespoons (45 ml) olive oil. Add the onions, bell pepper, and garlic, and cook, stirring occasionally, until soft and caramelized, about 15 minutes.

4. Stir in the cumin and cayenne and toast for 1 minute.

5. Add the tomatoes with their juices and cook until the tomatoes have thickened, about 10 minutes. Stir in the 1 teaspoon salt, 1 teaspoon pepper, basil leaves, and crumbled feta.

6. Remove the tomatoes from the oven and reduce the temperature to 375°F (190°C). Spoon the tomato sauce into the 8 roasted boats; you may have leftover sauce for dipping. Leave a little room in each tomato for the egg.

7. Gently crack an egg into each tomato and return the baking dish to the oven. Bake until the eggs are set, 7 to 10 minutes, depending on the desired degree of yolk doneness.

8. Serve immediately with warm pita bread for dipping.

Panzanella-Stuffed Tomato Boats

PREP TIME: 45 minutes
COOK TIME: 10 minutes
YIELD: serves 12 as a salad or side dish

Ingredients

BOATS
12 large globe tomatoes

FILLING
¼ cup (60 ml) extra-virgin
   olive oil
4 cups (140 g) cubed French bread
   (½-inch, or 13-mm, pieces)
1 English cucumber, seeded
   and diced
1 red bell pepper, seeded and diced
1 yellow bell pepper, seeded
   and diced
½ cup (80 g) diced red onion
1 cup (60 g) thinly sliced fresh
   basil leaves
¼ cup (34 g) rinsed and
   drained capers
½ teaspoon sea salt
½ teaspoon freshly ground
   black pepper

DRESSING
2 cloves garlic, minced
1 teaspoon Dijon mustard
1 teaspoon honey
¼ cup (60 ml) wine vinegar
½ teaspoon sea salt
½ teaspoon freshly ground
   black pepper
½ cup (120 ml) extra-virgin
   olive oil

continued

1. **To prepare the boats:** Slice a small piece off the bottom of each tomato, making a flat bottom. Cut off and reserve the top one-third of each tomato. Scoop out the seeds and pulp from each tomato and discard. Chop the reserved tops and set aside.

2. **To make the filling:** Heat the olive oil in a large skillet over medium heat. Add the bread and toast, stirring frequently until golden brown, about 10 minutes.

3. In a large bowl, combine the toasted bread, reserved chopped tomatoes, cucumber, bell peppers, onion, basil, capers, salt, and pepper.

4. **To make the dressing:** In a medium bowl, whisk together the garlic, Dijon, honey, vinegar, salt, and pepper. Slowly add in the olive oil, whisking vigorously until blended.

5. Pour the dressing over the salad and allow to marinate for 30 minutes.

6. Spoon the salad into the 12 boats and serve.

Southwestern Quinoa and Black Bean Baked Tomatoes

PREP TIME: 20 minutes
COOK TIME: 25 minutes
YIELD: serves 4 as a main course

Ingredients

4 large ripe tomatoes, whole, plus 1 large ripe tomato, diced, divided

2 tablespoons (30 ml) avocado or extra-virgin olive oil

2 cups (370 g) cooked quinoa

1 cup (6 ounces, or 172 g) canned black beans

1 teaspoon ground cumin

2 teaspoons chili powder

1 teaspoon garlic powder

1 teaspoon sweet paprika

1 teaspoon salt

½ cup (4.5 ounces, or 122 g) tomato sauce

1 cup (115 g) shredded Cheddar cheese

1. Preheat the oven to 375°F (190°C). Line a baking sheet with parchment paper.

2. With a sharp knife and a metal teaspoon, carefully cut a circle into each of the 4 whole tomatoes around the stem and scoop out the insides without piercing through the skin, leaving about ½-inch (13 mm) thickness around the skin to form the bowls. Set aside

3. In a large skillet over medium-high heat, heat the avocado oil. Add the diced tomato and cook for 3 to 4 minutes, stirring occasionally, until it starts to soften and is heated through.

4. Add the quinoa and black beans to the skillet, then stir in the cumin, chili powder, garlic powder, and paprika. Season with 1 teaspoon salt and lower the heat to medium. Continue to cook for 2 to 3 minutes more, tossing frequently.

5. Stir in the tomato sauce and cook for 3 to 4 minutes more. Remove from the heat.

6. Place the 4 boats on the prepared baking sheet and spoon the quinoa–black bean mixture into them, carefully packing in as much mixture as possible and mounding it over the tops. Press down on the mixture to form a flat surface on top for the cheese.

7. Top with the shredded cheese and bake for 12 to 14 minutes, until the cheese is melted. Serve immediately.

Zucchini Boats

Buffalo Chicken Zucchini Boats

PREP TIME: 20 minutes
COOK TIME: 45 minutes
YIELD: serves 3 as a main course

Ingredients

1 pound (454 g) boneless, skinless
   chicken breasts
Garlic powder
Salt and pepper, to taste
Extra-virgin olive oil, for drizzling
3 medium zucchini
1 cup (235 ml) Buffalo hot sauce,
   or to taste
½ cup (120 ml) blue cheese
   dressing
½ cup (60 g) crumbled blue cheese

1. Preheat the oven to 400°F (200°C). Line a baking sheet with parchment paper.

2. Season both sides of the chicken with garlic powder, salt, pepper, and a drizzle of olive oil. Place the seasoned chicken on the prepared baking sheet, transfer to the oven, and bake, turning once, until the chicken is fully cooked and light golden brown, 25 to 30 minutes. Set aside and let cool. Once cooled, slice and shred the chicken. Leave the oven on.

3. Slice the ends off each zucchini, then cut in half lengthwise. Carefully scoop out the flesh from the center of each half to form a cavity. Place each half, cut side up, on the baking sheet. Brush all sides with olive oil and sprinkle with salt. Transfer to the oven and bake for 5 minutes.

4. In a medium bowl, toss the chicken with as much (or as little) hot sauce as you like. Fill the 6 boats with a generous amount of the chicken mixture, return to the oven, and bake until the zucchini is tender, another 5 to 8 minutes. If desired, add a little extra hot sauce over the top.

5. Pour the blue cheese dressing into a squeeze bottle or into a small plastic sandwich bag. Cut the corner off the bag and drizzle the blue cheese dressing on top of the chicken. Top with the crumbled blue cheese and serve hot.

Thai Coconut Shrimp Zucchini Boats

TOTAL TIME: 30 minutes
YIELD: serves 4 as a main course

Ingredients
Nonstick cooking spray

BOATS
4 medium zucchini

FILLING
1 pound (454 g) rock shrimp, peeled
    and deveined
2 tablespoons (30 ml) coconut oil,
    melted and divided
2 cloves garlic, minced
¼ teaspoon kosher salt
½ teaspoon crushed red pepper flakes
1 cup (160 g) chopped yellow onion
1 cup (150 g) seeded and chopped
    red bell pepper
1 cup (150 g) seeded and chopped
    orange bell pepper

SAUCE
1 cup (235 ml) coconut milk
5 tablespoons (75 ml) fish sauce
1½ tablespoons (24 g) peanut butter
2 tablespoons (30 ml) freshly squeezed
    lime juice
1 tablespoon (12 g) light brown sugar
2 teaspoons ground ginger
2 tablespoons (8 g) chopped Thai basil
2 tablespoons (8 g) chopped cilantro
2 tablespoons (13 g) chopped scallion,
    for garnish
1 red jalapeño, thinly sliced, for garnish

1. Preheat the oven to 400°F (200°C). Spray a 9 × 13-inch (23 × 33 cm) baking dish with nonstick cooking spray.

2. **To prepare the boats:** Slice the ends off each zucchini, then cut in half lengthwise. Scoop out some of the flesh, leaving ¼ inch (6 mm) around the sides. Reserve the flesh for another use. Place the zucchini boats in the prepared baking dish and transfer to the oven. Bake until tender, 25 to 30 minutes.

3. **To make the filling:** While the zucchini cooks, in a large bowl, combine the shrimp with 1 tablespoon (15 ml) of the coconut oil, the garlic, salt, and crushed red pepper. Set aside.

4. Heat the remaining 1 tablespoon (15 ml) coconut oil in a large skillet over medium-high heat. Add the onion and bell peppers, and cook, stirring occasionally, for about 5 minutes. Once the onions and peppers are tender, add the shrimp and cook, stirring occasionally, until the shrimp are pink, 2 to 3 minutes.

5. **To make the sauce:** In a medium bowl, whisk together the coconut milk, fish sauce, peanut butter, lime juice, brown sugar, and ginger. Pour the sauce over the shrimp mixture and bring to a boil. Reduce the heat to medium-low and simmer for 2 minutes.

6. Remove from the heat, check the seasonings, and then stir in the basil and cilantro.

7. Divide the mixture among the 8 boats. Top with the scallion and sliced jalapeño.

Turkish Rice and Lamb-Stuffed Zucchini with Yogurt Sauce

PREP TIME: 20 minutes
COOK TIME: 50 minutes
YIELD: serves 4 as a main course or 8 as a starter or side

Ingredients

FILLING
1 tablespoon (15 ml) olive oil
1 cup (160 g) diced sweet onion
2 cloves garlic, minced
½ pound (225 g) ground lamb
½ cup (48 g) medium-grain rice
2 tablespoons (18 g) dried currants
1 tablespoon (9 g) pine nuts
½ teaspoon ground allspice
½ teaspoon ground cinnamon
½ teaspoon ground cloves
2 tablespoons (8 g) chopped
   fresh parsley
1 teaspoon chopped mint
Salt and pepper, to taste

BOATS
4 medium zucchini

TOMATO SAUCE
1 can (14.5 ounces, or 411 g)
   diced tomatoes
1½ cups (355 ml) hot water
2 tablespoons (30 ml) freshly
   squeezed lemon juice
1 tablespoon (15 ml) sugar

YOGURT SAUCE
1 cup (230 g) nonfat Greek yogurt
1 tablespoon (6 g) lemon zest
2 tablespoons (30 ml) freshly
   squeezed lemon juice
Salt and pepper, to taste

1. **To make the filling:** Heat the olive oil in a large skillet over medium heat. Add the onion and cook and stir until tender, about 4 minutes. Stir in the garlic.

2. Add the lamb and cook, stirring occasionally, until browned, 5 to 7 minutes. Drain the excess fat.

3. Stir in the rice, currants, pine nuts, allspice, cinnamon, cloves, parsley, and mint. Season with salt and pepper.

4. **To make the boats:** Trim the stems from the zucchini, then cut in half lengthwise. Scoop out the flesh of the zucchini, maintaining ½ inch (13 mm) around the sides. Place the zucchini boats into a large, deep pan.

5. Fill the 8 zucchini boats with the meat mixture.

6. **To make the tomato sauce:** In a medium bowl, combine the diced tomatoes, hot water, lemon juice, and sugar. Pour over the zucchini boats. The liquid should come up to just underneath the filling.

7. Bring the mixture to a boil over medium-high heat, reduce the heat to medium-low, cover, and simmer for 30 to 40 minutes, basting occasionally with the juices.

8. **To make the yogurt sauce:** Meanwhile, in a medium bowl, combine the yogurt, lemon zest, and lemon juice, and season with salt and pepper. Refrigerate until ready to serve.

9. Allow the zucchini to cool completely and then serve drizzled with the yogurt sauce.

Zucchini, Lemon, and Pecorino Romano Risotto Zucchini Boats

PREP TIME: 20 minutes
COOK TIME: 50 minutes
YIELD: serves 8 as a side dish

Ingredients
5 medium zucchini, divided
Nonstick cooking spray
Salt and pepper, to taste
6 cups (1.4 L) chicken or vegetable stock
1 tablespoon (15 g) unsalted butter
2 tablespoons (30 ml) olive oil
2 large shallots, minced
2 cloves garlic, minced
2 cups (390 g) Arborio rice
½ cup (120 ml) dry white wine
1 cup (100 g) grated Pecorino Romano cheese
2 tablespoons (12 g) lemon zest
2 tablespoons (30 ml) freshly squeezed lemon juice
¼ cup (15 g) chopped fresh basil

1. Preheat the oven to 400°F (200°C). Line a baking sheet with parchment paper.

2. To prepare the zucchini boats, slice the ends from 4 of the zucchini, cut in half lengthwise, and scoop out some of the flesh, leaving ¼ inch (6 mm) around the sides. Chop the scooped-out flesh and chop the remaining zucchini. Set aside.

3. Transfer the zucchini boats to the prepared baking sheet, spray them with nonstick cooking spray, and season with salt and pepper. Transfer to the oven and bake until tender and lightly browned, 20 to 25 minutes.

4. Meanwhile, in a medium saucepan over high heat, bring the chicken stock to a boil, reduce the heat to low, and keep warm.

5. In a large, deep, heavy-bottomed pan, heat the butter and olive oil over medium heat. Add the shallots and reserved chopped zucchini, and cook and stir until tender, about 5 minutes. Stir in the garlic.

6. Add the rice and stir to coat with the oil mixture. Add the wine and stir until evaporated, about 1 minute.

7. Add 1½ cups (355 ml) of the hot stock and stir the risotto until the liquid is absorbed. Continue adding in remaining liquid, ½ cup (120 ml) at a time, until all the stock is absorbed, about 35 to 45 minutes. Stir frequently.

8. Turn off the heat, add in the cheese, lemon zest, lemon juice, and basil, and season with salt and pepper.

9. To serve, spoon the risotto into the 8 cooked boats.

Zucchini Taco Boats

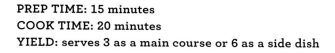

PREP TIME: 15 minutes
COOK TIME: 20 minutes
YIELD: serves 3 as a main course or 6 as a side dish

Ingredients

3 medium zucchini

Olive oil, for brushing

Salt and pepper, to taste

1 pound (454 g) ground beef,
    chicken, or turkey

¼ cup (35 g) taco seasoning

1 cup (8 ounces, or 245 g)
    tomato sauce

½ cup (90 g) chopped tomato

1¼ cups (145 g) shredded Cheddar
    cheese

¼ cup (25 g) chopped scallion,
    for garnish

Handful fresh cilantro, roughly
    chopped, for garnish

1. Preheat the oven to 400°F (200°C). Line a baking sheet with parchment paper.

2. Slice the ends off each of the zucchini, then cut in half lengthwise. Carefully scoop out the flesh from the center of each half to form a cavity. Place each half, cut side up, on the prepared baking sheet. Brush each side with olive oil and sprinkle with salt. Transfer to the oven and bake for 5 minutes.

3. Meanwhile, heat a large skillet over medium-high heat. Add the meat and season with the taco seasoning, and salt and pepper. Cook, stirring occasionally, until browned. Drain any excess oil from the meat.

4. After removing the zucchini from the oven, set the oven to broil. Scoop the meat mixture into the 6 boats. Top with as much tomato sauce, chopped tomato, and shredded Cheddar cheese as you like. You may add additional items like black beans, jalapeños, or olives, if desired. Place back into the oven and broil until the cheese is melted, 5 to 8 minutes. Top with the scallion and cilantro.

Zucchini Pizza Boats

PREP TIME: 20 minutes
COOK TIME: 15 minutes
YIELD: serves 3 as main course or 6 as a side dish

Ingredients
3 medium zucchini
Olive oil, for brushing
Salt and pepper, to taste
1 pound (454 g) ground beef,
    chicken, or turkey
1 teaspoon garlic powder
1 cup (8 ounces, or 245 g)
    tomato sauce
1¼ cups (140 g) shredded
    mozzarella cheese
Dried oregano
Pepperoni, olives, or any of your
    favorite pizza toppings

1. Preheat the oven to 400°F (200°C). Line a baking sheet with parchment paper.

2. Slice the ends off each of the zucchini, then cut them in half lengthwise. Carefully scoop out the seedy flesh from the center of each zucchini to form a cavity. Place each half, cut side up, on the prepared baking sheet, and brush all over with olive oil. Sprinkle with salt, transfer to the oven, bake for 5 minutes, and then set aside. Leave the oven on.

3. Meanwhile, heat a medium skillet over medium-high heat. Add the ground beef and season with the garlic powder and salt and pepper. Cook, stirring occasionally, until browned. Drain the excess fat.

4. Set the oven to broil. Scoop the meat mixture into the 6 baked boats. Spoon the tomato sauce on top, and then sprinkle with the mozzarella cheese. Sprinkle with the oregano and then add your favorite toppings.

5. Return the zucchini to the oven and broil until the cheese is melted and the toppings begin to get toasty, for 5 to 8 minutes. Cool and serve as a side dish or a meal.

Zucchini Tuna Melts

PREP TIME: 20 minutes
COOK TIME: 25 minutes
YIELD: serves 2 as a main course or 4 as a snack

Ingredients
2 large zucchini
Nonstick cooking spray
Salt and pepper, to taste
1 can (5 ounces, or 140 g) tuna, drained
1 small plum tomato, chopped
2 tablespoons (20 g) chopped red onion
2 tablespoons (8 g) chopped fresh parsley
1 teaspoon garlic powder
½ teaspoon black pepper
1 teaspoon red wine vinegar
1 teaspoon olive oil
1 cup (115 g) shredded Cheddar cheese
½ cup (50 g) grated Parmesan cheese, or to taste

1. Preheat the oven to 400°F (200°C). Line a baking sheet with parchment paper.

2. Slice the ends off each of the zucchini, then cut them in half lengthwise. Carefully scoop out the flesh from the center of each half to form a cavity.

3. Place the zucchini, side by side, on the prepared baking sheet, spray both sides of each zucchini with nonstick cooking spray, and sprinkle with salt and pepper. Transfer to the oven and bake for 20 minutes. Let cool for about 5 minutes. Leave the oven on.

4. While the zucchini bake, make the tuna. In a medium bowl, flake the tuna with a fork. Add the chopped tomato, onion, parsley, garlic powder, pepper, vinegar, and olive oil, and combine well.

5. Set the oven to broil. Fill the 4 cooled boats with a heaping amount of the tuna mixture. Top with the Cheddar cheese, then sprinkle with the Parmesan. Return to the oven and broil until the cheese is melted and tops are slightly toasty, 5 to 6 minutes.

Fruit Boats

Chia Pudding Papaya Boats

TOTAL TIME: overnight plus 15 minutes
YIELD: serves 2 as a breakfast

Ingredients
1 cup (235 ml) vanilla almond milk
¼ cup (48 g) chia seeds
1 tablespoon (20 g) raw honey
1 teaspoon vanilla extract
1 ripe medium-to-large papaya
½ cup (75 g) blueberries
¼ cup (31 g) toasted almond slices
¼ cup (18 g) toasted coconut flakes

1. The night before serving this breakfast, combine the almond milk, chia seeds, honey, and vanilla extract in a jar, and shake vigorously. Store in the refrigerator overnight.

2. The next day, cut the papaya in half lengthwise and scoop out the seeds.

3. Remove the chia pudding from the refrigerator and fill each boat with the pudding.

4. Arrange the blueberries, almonds, and coconut on top.

Almond-Coconut Açai Boats

TOTAL TIME: 15 minutes
YIELD: serves 2 as a breakfast

Ingredients

2 packages (3.5 ounces, or
    100 grams, each) frozen
    unsweetened açai
1 frozen banana
1 cup (245 g) frozen pineapple
1 cup (235 ml) unsweetened
    almond milk
1 coconut, halved
½ cup (61 g) granola
¼ cup (18 g) toasted coconut flakes
1 cup (125 g) fresh berries, such
    as raspberries, blueberries,
    or blackberries

1. Combine the açai, banana, pineapple, and almond milk in a
    blender. Puree until smooth.

2. Pour the smoothie into the coconut boats and top with the
    granola, coconut flakes, and berries. Serve immediately.

Watermelon, Tomato, Arugula, and Feta Salad in Watermelon Boats

TOTAL TIME: 20 minutes
YIELD: serves 4 as a salad

Ingredients

2 seedless baby watermelons

1 pint (300 g) heirloom cherry or grape tomatoes, halved

1 container (5 ounces, or 142 g) baby wild arugula

3 ounces (85 g) sheep's milk feta, crumbled

½ cup (30 g) torn basil leaves

¼ cup (60 ml) balsamic reduction or glaze

2 tablespoons (30 ml) extra-virgin olive oil

1. Cut each watermelon in half through the middle. Scoop out all of the pulp, leaving 4 perfect boats behind. Cut a little bit off the bottom of each half so that the watermelon boats are stable on a flat surface.

2. Chop the watermelon pulp into bite-size pieces.

3. To assemble the salad, layer the watermelon pulp and tomatoes in the 4 boats. Top with the arugula, feta, and basil. Drizzle with the balsamic reduction and olive oil, and serve immediately.

Yogurt, Berry, and Granola Cantaloupe Boats

TOTAL TIME: 20 minutes
YIELD: serves 2 as a breakfast

Ingredients

1 large ripe cantaloupe (you can
   substitute honeydew)
1 cup (110 g) strawberries,
   tops removed and sliced
2 cups (480 g) plain full-fat Greek
   yogurt
½ cup (73 g) blueberries
1 cup (122 g) granola of choice
¼ cup (24 g) fresh mint leaves,
   roughly chopped, for garnish

1. On a hard surface with a sharp knife, carefully cut the cantaloupe in half. Scoop out the seeds with a metal spoon and discard. With a melon baller, scoop out the cantaloupe, leaving about ¾ inch (2 cm) of melon around the rims and bottoms to create bowls. Reserve the melon balls and set aside.

2. Fill each boat with one-quarter of the reserved melon balls and the strawberries. Cover the fruit with the yogurt. Top the yogurt with the remaining strawberries and melon, along with the blueberries.

3. Top with the granola and garnish with the mint. Serve immediately.

Wheatberry Cinnamon Baked Apple Boats

PREP TIME: 15 minutes
COOK TIME: 20 minutes
YIELD: serves 4 to 8 as a dessert

Ingredients
4 Honeycrisp apples
2 to 3 tablespoons (15 to 45 ml)
    ground cinnamon, divided
Coconut oil spray
2 cups cooked hard red
    wheatberries (see Note, below)
1 cup (117 g) chopped walnuts
1 cup (145 g) golden raisins
1 cup (100 g) confectioners' sugar

*Note: Add 1 cup (195 g) wheatberries
to 2½ cups (600 ml) boiling water,
reduce the heat to a simmer, cover,
and cook until liquid is absorbed,
about 25 minutes.*

1. Preheat the oven to 375°F (190°C). Line a baking sheet with aluminum foil.

2. Slice each apple evenly in half lengthwise through the top. With a metal teaspoon, carefully scoop out the seeds and insides, without piercing through the skin, to form bowls.

3. Place the apples on the prepared baking sheet, sprinkle them with the desired amount of cinnamon, and spray with the coconut oil spray. Bake for 15 minutes, then remove from the oven.

4. Meanwhile, in a medium bowl, add the wheatberries, walnuts, raisins, the remaining desired amount of cinnamon, and ¾ cup (75 g) of the confectioners' sugar. Combine well.

5. Stuff the 8 boats with as much filling as possible. Return them to the oven and bake for 5 minutes, until heated through.

6. Remove from the oven and transfer to a serving dish. Dust the bowls with the remaining ¼ cup (25 g) confectioners' sugar. Serve immediately.

Watermelon-Tomato Gazpacho in Watermelon Boats

TOTAL TIME: 2 hours 20 minutes
YIELD: serves 2 as a light meal or 4 as a starter

Ingredients

2 seedless baby watermelons
5 large beefsteak tomatoes, roughly chopped
1 English cucumber, roughly chopped
1 clove garlic, peeled
½ jalapeño pepper
4 sprigs basil
4 sprigs cilantro, washed and leaves picked
1 teaspoon sea salt
2 tablespoons (30 ml) sherry vinegar
1 tablespoon (15 ml) extra-virgin olive oil
½ cup (70 g) diced cucumber, for garnish
¼ cup (15 g) thinly sliced fresh basil, for garnish

1. Cut each watermelon in half through the middle. Scoop out all of the pulp, leaving 4 perfect bowls behind. Cut a little bit off the bottom of each half so that the watermelon boats are stable on a flat surface. Refrigerate the boats until ready to use.

2. Working in batches, puree the watermelon pulp, tomatoes, roughly chopped cucumber, garlic, jalapeño, basil sprigs, cilantro leaves, salt, sherry vinegar, and olive oil in a blender until smooth and creamy. Transfer the pureed soup to a large bowl. Cover, refrigerate, and allow the flavors to meld for at least 2 hours.

3. When ready to serve, ladle the soup into the 4 prepared watermelon boats and top with the diced cucumber and sliced basil.

Chicken Cashew Curry in Coconut Boats

PREP TIME: 2 hours 20 minutes
COOK TIME: 15 minutes
YIELD: serves 4 as a main course

Ingredients

CHICKEN

2 pounds (907 g) boneless, skinless
  chicken breasts
2 teaspoons curry powder
2 teaspoons garam masala
½ teaspoon salt
2 tablespoons (30 g) ghee,
  melted

SAUCE

1 sweet onion, quartered
2 medium tomatoes, quartered
2 cloves garlic, peeled
1 tablespoon (15 g) ghee
1 tablespoon (15 ml) curry powder
1 teaspoon ground coriander

1 teaspoon garam masala
¼ teaspoon crushed red
  pepper flakes
2 teaspoons raw sugar
1 cup (150 g) roasted cashews
½ cup (120 ml) water
1 can (14 ounces, or 425 ml)
  coconut milk
½ cup (115 g) Greek yogurt
2 cups (330 g) cooked basmati
  rice

BOATS

2 coconuts, halved
½ cup (30 g) chopped fresh
  cilantro, for garnish

continued

1. **To make the chicken:** In a large bowl, massage the chicken with the curry powder, garam masala, salt, and ghee. Cover, refrigerate, and allow to marinate for at least 2 hours, but preferably overnight.

2. Heat a grill over medium-high heat. Once hot, place the chicken breasts on the grill and cook until charred and cooked through, 6 to 7 minutes per side. Transfer to a cutting board, let rest for 5 minutes, and then cut into bite-size pieces.

3. **To make the sauce:** While the chicken is cooking, make the sauce. In a blender, combine the onion, tomato, and garlic. Puree until smooth, about 1 minute.

4. In a large, deep skillet, heat the ghee over medium heat. Add the onion-tomato mixture and allow to simmer for 5 minutes. Stir in the curry powder, coriander, garam masala, red pepper flakes, and sugar.

5. Add the cashews, water, coconut milk, and yogurt. Bring to a simmer and cook, stirring occasionally, for an additional 5 to 7 minutes.

6. Add the cooked chicken and continue to cook for 2 minutes more.

7. **To assemble the boats:** Spoon rice into the 4 boats, top with the coconut-cashew chicken, and sprinkle with cilantro.

INDEX

Photograph by Erika Krumm

ABOUT THE AUTHOR

Marlena Kur is an avid food lover and creator of the hugely popular Instagram Zest My Lemon (@zestmylemon), which she launched in 2015. Her creative dishes are loaded with simple, nourishing ingredients for clean, delicious eating and healthy living. Based in Levittown, New York, Marlena is a full-time mother, blogger, influencer, and natural foods ambassador for a variety of brands and businesses. She can be reached at zestmylemon.com.